The
Circular Church

The Circular Church

THREE CENTURIES OF CHARLESTON HISTORY

JOANNE CALHOUN

Charleston · London
History
PRESS

Published by The History Press
Charleston, SC 29403
www.historypress.net

Copyright © 2008 by Joanne Calhoun
All rights reserved

Cover design by Marshall Hudson.

First published 2008

Manufactured in the United Kingdom

ISBN 978.1.59629.359.5

Library of Congress Cataloging-in-Publication Data

Calhoun, Joanne.
The Circular Church : three centuries of Charleston history / Joanne
Calhoun in collaboration with Pat Spaulding ... [et al.].
p. cm.
Includes bibliographical references (p.   ) and index.
ISBN-13: 978-1-59629-359-5 (alk. paper)
1. Independent or Congregational Church of Charleston, South
Carolina--History. 2. Charleston (S.C.)--Church history. I. Title.
BX7255.C36C35 2007
285.8'757915--dc22

2007045066

CONTENTS

PREFACE

To commemorate the 325th anniversary of the Circular Congregational Church, a committee of church members decided to write an updated and accessible history of one of the oldest congregations in Charleston. We felt lucky to be part of such an incredibly rich history, and felt that there was a wealth of stories that would be of interest to our members and friends as well as to the large number of visitors who tour our church and its graveyard. We wondered about the roles of women and African Americans in our history, and about how the political, social and economic culture of the times affected the congregations. We wanted a book that could serve as a guide to the church's history, building and graveyard. We also wanted to find out more about the individuals who lived this history. We tried to include those people and details that were historically significant or representative and those that were unique, interesting or important to the spirit of the church. To facilitate using this book as a guide to the graveyard and to Charleston, we included a graveyard guide and a numbered map of the area of Charleston correlated with places and events in the book. Captions for many of the images in this book include a letter or number designation (A1, A2, B, C or D). These numbers relate to the Circular Church graveyard map found in Appendix A. Please see page 171 to locate particular gravestones.

A book by committee seems especially appropriate for a Congregational church because the Congregational form of governance is, as the name suggests, by the congregation (and usually by committee), as opposed to by the clergy or the hierarchy. This system makes each Congregational church independent and unique, and is important to understanding some of the incidents that occur in Circular's history, especially for readers who come from a more hierarchical religious background.

As we wrote we came to more fully understand the strengths and courage of the people who founded our church in 1681. We also came to appreciate more the similarities of these people to ourselves and our problems, as well as the incredible things they accomplished against all obstacles. Building the addition to Lance Hall in 2006 was a huge undertaking for the present congregation; in comparison, the original church members settled a colony, built a church, survived plagues and hurricanes and built personal fortunes all at the same time.

The people of the second church on this site, still called the Independent Meeting House, exemplified the progression of the Dissenter spirit. Led by their minister, William Tennent, they played a major role in the American Revolution. The church flourished during the period after the Revolution, as did Charleston and the rest of South Carolina, and a large circular structure was completed in 1806. In 1861, a terrible fire destroyed much of Charleston, including Old Circular Church. Due to the economic conditions left by the Civil War, a new sanctuary was not built on the site until 1892. This was the smaller Circular Church, which stands on the site today.

Since the Independent Meeting House of 1681 was home to most Dissenters of the time, several Charleston churches were formed from its membership as the population of Charleston increased. First (Scots) Presbyterian, the French Huguenot Church and the Unitarian Church were formed by members who worshipped at the Independent Church. The period after the Civil War also saw black members leave Circular to form Plymouth Congregational Church.

Originally, the church was completely independent from any one denomination. English Congregationalists, Scots Presbyterians and French Huguenots, all of whom came to this country as religious Dissenters, banded together to erect one meetinghouse known as the White Meeting House or the Independent Meeting House. Ministers were usually Congregational from England or New England, or Presbyterian from Scotland. The congregations insisted through the years that the church remain independent of either of these denominations and that the "pastors not try to alter that independency." It was not until 1882 that the Independent or Circular Church joined the Congregational Association in order to get support for the church, which struggled after the fire of 1861 and the Civil War. In 1954, Circular continued its membership when this organization became the United Church of Christ. In 1968, Circular joined the Atlantic Presbytery of the United Presbyterian Church (USA). Circular is one of the few congregations in the South that expresses its ecumenical commitment by belonging to two denominations, supporting the national and international ministries of both, but retaining its independence.

The congregation of Circular continues to be very active in the community today and looks to the future as well as the past. We hope this book will help members and friends to be aware of the role the church has played in Charleston and in South Carolina, and to come to realize, as we have, that we are part of an extraordinary tradition.

Circular History Committee:
Joanne Calhoun
Paul Calhoun
Lisa Hayes
David Rison
Elaine Simpson
Pat Spaulding

ACKNOWLEDGEMENTS

In the fall of 2006, the idea for this book was born out of a meeting at which Rev. Bert Keller shared stories of the history of the church. In typical Congregational mode, we called together a group of people who might enjoy working on a book to commemorate the church's 325th anniversary. A few of us decided to take it on. From then on it became a "book by committee." Pat Spaulding, Circular's archivist, contributed the majority of facts and tidbits that constitute this history. David Rison, retired chair of the History Department at Charleston Southern University, whose area of expertise is twentieth-century Southern history, added many other facts and ideas, checked sources, worked on the index and bibliography and kept us scholarly. Lisa Hayes, librarian of the South Carolina Historical Society, was an invaluable reference source, added some very interesting stories, obtained many rare images for us and drew the maps. Elaine Simpson, a longtime member and past president of Circular, was the expert on the most recent thirty years of the church and helped a great deal with pictures and with keeping things flowing. It was my husband, Paul Calhoun's, idea to write the book; he initiated the effort and he was invaluable in helping with anything technical, be it images or computer problems. I served as author and editor, putting together the ideas that others contributed, finding a few on my own and then weaving it together with a narrative. All of us met biweekly for five months and then weekly for four months. All of us proofread and edited. All of us enjoyed it and grew to think of each other as "book family."

The committee would like to thank all of those people who gave us help and encouragement in a variety of ways. First of all, photographers Missy Loewe, Ron Rocz and Natalie Simpson, all professionals, gave us most of the wonderful photographs that make this book special. Their generosity was unbelievable.

Bert Keller contributed several pieces for the fourth church section and proofread an early draft. His gentle prodding led to a better narrative. Steve Hoffius did an interview, lent his resources and expertise, and encouraged us. Barbara Cole, Susan Dunn, Bruce Jayne, Lucille Keller, JoAnne Marcel, Marilyn Taylor and Joan Young also contributed. Frieda McDuffy shared her ideas and passed along a compilation of some past research documentation by a former member, Denise Rankin, which was helpful. Alli Campbell helped with picture placement and classification. Kaye and Bill Sharpe served as resident experts for the fourth church section, as did Mary Thomas. We owe an incredible debt to the late Rev. George Edwards, former pastor of Circular Church. Without the six years of research included in his book on the first 250 years of church history, this book would not have been possible. David Mould and Missy Loewe's book on Charleston's graveyards was also an invaluable resource. Shelene Roumillat's paper on the African Americans of Circular in the nineteenth century was very enlightening. Our editor, Lee Handford of the History Press, was patient, understanding and encouraging. We are also grateful to the South Carolina Historical Society for its generosity in sharing its resources.

Special thanks go to the last group of stalwarts who did proofreading for us, sometimes twice. They are Kim Calhoun, Paul Calhoun Jr., Karen and Karl Faller, Lilla Folsom, Rev. Bert Keller, Sheila Mable, the Rev. Erick Olsen and Susan Rison.

HISTORICAL BACKGROUND

From its beginning 327 years ago, the story of Circular Church has been attached to the history of Charleston, to South Carolina and to the nation. The congregation was organized in Charleston as the original "Dissenter" (Protestant, non-Anglican) church in the colony. It was known as the Independent or the White Meeting House, as only Anglican churches at that time could use the designation "church." Members of the congregation included English Congregationalists, Scotch Presbyterians and French Huguenots. In the early years of the colony, the only other Charleston church was St. Philip's (Anglican Church of England), which was also founded in 1681. (Until after the Revolution, Charleston was spelled "Charles Towne" or "Charles Town." We chose to use the modern spelling throughout for uniformity.)

The Lords Proprietors of the Carolina colony, hoping to attract nonconforming settlers, guaranteed "full and free liberty of Conscience" to all settlers. Attracted by this promise of religious freedom, Dissenters came in great numbers. By 1685, the colony's population was 2,500; a portion was of the Established Church of England, but a large majority were Dissenters.[1]

Conflict soon began between the Anglicans and the Dissenters. The Anglican settlers of Goose Creek rejected the Lords Proprietors' policy of religious tolerance that the Dissenters supported. In 1700 the Proprietors sought a compromise, but in 1704 the governor and the assembly passed a Test Act that refused Dissenters the right to serve in the legislature and an Establishment Act that made the Church of England the official church in the colony. The Dissenters complained to the English Parliament, hiring Daniel Defoe (author of *Robinson Crusoe*) to support them. Defoe wrote a pamphlet that swayed public opinion in England in the Dissenters' favor. The House of Lords agreed with the Dissenters, and the Privy Council

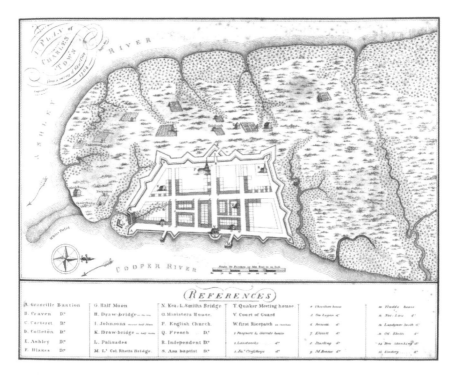

Crisp Map of 1704. *Courtesy South Carolina Historical Society.*

ordered the South Carolina Assembly to repeal the two measures, which it did. In 1706, however, the legislature passed the Church Act, which made the Anglican Church the official, tax-supported church of the colony. In a spirit of compromise, the legislature also passed the Establishment Act of 1706 providing Dissenters full political rights.

Members of the Independent Meeting House could only worship in their own way by sacrificing to build and maintain their meetinghouse as well as paying the official Church Tax for support of the Anglican Church. Thus from its beginning, the determined congregation forged a tradition of challenging the established order, a tradition that has continued throughout its history. In 1706, thirty-six years after Charleston was established, the Rev. Edward Marston, then rector of St. Philip's Church, said that the Dissenters (in Charleston) constituted about two-thirds of the population. He also said, "they are the soberest, the most numerous, and richest people of the Province."[2]

1.

FIRST CHURCH BUILDING, 1681 TO 1732

The Dissenters erected their first meetinghouse in the far northwest corner of the walled city of Charleston, "at the beginning of the settlement."[3] The present sanctuary occupies the exact site. A square building, forty feet on a side, the original church was popularly called the "White Meeting House," owing to its color.[4] It was also known as the Meeting House, or simply, the Meeting; Meeting Street was named after it. Education was available at the Congregationalist School, established in the 1690s, where Matthew Bee taught until the yellow fever carried him off in 1699,[5] but no other references are made to this school. Because the earliest church records were destroyed in a hurricane, we have little information about the founding members of the church, but occasional details of their lives and personalities emerge from their tombstones and other existing records.

MINISTERS

The little information we have about the early ministers of the Independent Meeting House of Charleston gives glimpses of the hardships of their lives, which were often cut short by disease. Their backgrounds also reveal the church's close ties with New England, England and Scotland. In 1691, the Rev. Benjamin Pierpont migrated from Boston to found an Independent church in Charleston. He died in 1698, and the Rev. Hugh Adams took his place. On his arrival, he found the plague raging, far worse than the Great Plague of London, considering the smallness of the town. Shops closed for six weeks; little was done in town but carrying medicines, digging graves and carting the dead. While Rev. Adams survived, he suffered from "Putrid Feaver, Dropsie, Scurvy, Pestilence and Hypocondriack Melancholy." He credited the Lord's blessing for his cures. Adams was a controversial and rather ineffective figure; he was always in hot water and was very explosive over such points as whether magistrates should wear wigs and whether Sunday should be called the Sabbath.

The Rev. John Cotton Jr., son of the distinguished minister Rev. John Cotton of Boston and uncle of the famous New England minister Cotton Mather, came to the White Meeting House in 1698, after having served a thirty-year pastorate in the original Pilgrim Church at Plymouth. Before that he was a missionary to the Native Americans. Because he was fluent in their languages, he helped in the revision of the Indian Bible and other manuscripts for publication. Rev. Cotton died of yellow fever just a little over six months after his settlement in Charleston.

One of the most interesting glimpses into many of the problems during these early years is seen in the tenure of Rev. Archibald Stobo. His story has all of the ingredients of Charleston life during this period: a hurricane, miraculous coincidence, luck, ego, humor, politics, religious dedication, conviction, tension and a vision for the future. A minister of the Church of Scotland, Stobo was called to the pulpit of the White Meeting House by a very indirect route. He left Scotland in August of 1699 bound for Darien, a new Scottish colony established near what is today the Caribbean entrance to the Panama Canal. Stobo and his fellow travelers were not met warmly by either the Spanish or the natives and they quickly abandoned the colony.

Rev. Stobo, his family and some of the 1,300 Scottish settlers sailed the *Rising Sun* from Darien bound for Scotland. The ship arrived in Charleston Harbor in September of 1700 seeking supplies and rest. Hearing of the vessel's inhabitants, and having lost their previous minister in September of 1699 to yellow fever, White Meeting House congregants went down to the ship and induced Stobo to come ashore to preach for them the next day. He agreed, and shortly after he disembarked the ship with his family and twelve other Scots, a fierce hurricane slammed into the area, sinking the *Rising Sun*, her crew and passengers. Stobo would judge the event as punishment for the behavior of the ship's crew, believing they were rude company and sinners of the highest order, and he wrote to a colleague later that "the ship's crew were so filled with wickedness that 'they could hold no more; they were ripe, they must be cut down with the sickle of his wrath.'"[6] He was much more concerned by the loss of his books than of the crew.[7] He and his family lost all of their possessions except his pocket Bible, which is now housed at the South Carolina Historical Society in Charleston.

Rev. Stobo was renowned as an orator, and his sermons lasted for many (four plus) hours. Church officers asked that he divide his sermons into two sessions so that members could break for the usual dinner hour. He refused, and the next Sunday Solomon Legare and his family got up to leave as the

Stobo Bible. *Courtesy South Carolina Historical Society.*

clock struck twelve. As they silently walked down the aisle of the church, Rev. Stobo called out in a loud Scottish accent, "Aye, aye, a little petcher is soon full!" Legare replied, "You've said enough to fill all the cisterns in Charleston," and went on his way.[8]

In an early incident demonstrating the Congregational style of governance, the congregation asked Stobo to leave after four years of his ministry because he was too strongly Presbyterian in his teachings to suit the Congregational and Huguenot members. He went on to become known as "the Father of Presbyterianism" in the Lowcountry because under his guidance and supervision five Lowcountry Presbyterian churches were founded, among them the still thriving James Island Presbyterian Church. He was an outspoken opponent of the Church Act and worked for its repeal throughout the colony.[9]

In 1704, William Livingston, who was born in Ireland, immigrated to Charleston and was pastor until his death in 1720. It was from Rev. Livingston's house on White Point in 1713 that the records of the church were lost in a hurricane. The violent storm "beat off the weatherboards of the house, carried away the book that contained the church records and the furniture of the rooms on the lower floor."[10] Peter Bart, a black man, waited on Rev. Livingston and was with him at the time of the hurricane. Both narrowly escaped its ravages. Thomas Lamboll, a clerk of the church for forty years, recalled that 1713 hurricane, which occurred when he was nineteen:

> *On September 5 came on the great hurricane which was attended with such an Inundation from the sea and to such an unknown height that a*

Simonds Family Brick Vault, the oldest tomb structure in Charleston. The vault contains the bodies of Henry Simonds, 1695, his wife Frances and their son. *Courtesy Natalie Simpson* (A1).

great many lives were lost; all the vessels in Charleston harbor, except one, were drove ashore. The new Look-out on Sullivan's Island, of wood, built eight square and eighty feet high, blown down; all the front wall and mud parapet before Charlestowne undermined and washed away.[11]

MEMBERS OF NOTE

Even though records of this period are scarce, we do know that members of the early church were from diverse backgrounds and occupations. They were some of the most influential political, economic and military leaders in the colony. Gravestones are our chief source of reference for these people. Included in this section is a sampling of the founding members who represent aspects of the church and of life in Charleston at the time.

The oldest unmarked vault in Charleston contains the graves of Henry Simons, Simonds or Symons (spellings vary) and his family. Henry and his wife, Frances, gave the land for the original church building. Her will of 1707 contained the following clause: "I will that a Cedar Plank be laid on my Husband's Grave, and one on my Son's; & when I shall be buried, that the open place of the burial-place shall be walled up with Brick."[12]

The graves of the John Dart family tell a story typical of the times. John Dart was a prominent member of the congregation who achieved success

John Dart family. *Courtesy Natalie Simpson* (A1).

as a merchant and a lawyer. He was also a leading member of the local assembly. Prominence did not make life easy, however. He married three times. Childbirth, malaria and smallpox took their toll on women in those early days. The gravestones show that five of his daughters died by age six.[13]

Miles Brewton, another founder of the church and a member of a prominent Charleston family, emigrated from Barbados in 1684 and became a goldsmith, a banker and a militia officer. His more famous grandson, also Miles, became quite prosperous. Young Miles's education in England emphasizes how wealthy a family of this time could become in two generations. His connections to the family businesses prepared him to amass a vast fortune and he became very influential politically.

The Legares are an example of an early family whose large fortune was made as planters and merchants. Solomon Legare fled papal persecution in France, as he was a Huguenot. He married an English woman, an act that displeased his father, who gave him twenty shillings and cut him out of his will. Solomon immigrated to South Carolina accompanied by his wife, his mother and other relatives. He was a jeweler and gold and silversmith. In 1729, he bought a small island contiguous to Folly Island, which still bears his name. He also owned large tracts of real estate at Legare and Tradd Streets. He served on the grand jury that convicted and hanged Stede Bonnet, the pirate. His mother was the first adult buried in the Circular

Miles Brewton House, 27 King Street. *Courtesy Paul Calhoun.*

Church graveyard, but her grave was covered when a newer, larger church was built.[14] His wife's gravestone and his footstone are visible today. Solomon Legare's daughter, Sarah, married Solomon Freer, whose family came from Barbados and made up part of Charleston's elite. She died of smallpox, as did so many, in the epidemics common in Charleston. Her headstone "is one of the best-preserved slate stones bearing an old-style winged death's head."[15] It disappeared for a while from the graveyard, and was featured in a newspaper article of missing gravestones. Someone who read the article found the gravestone in a house in Columbia, South Carolina, and it was returned in 1988.[16]

The Peronneaus were an influential Huguenot family in the early church. Henry Peronneau was born in 1667 in La Rochelle, France, and arrived in Charleston in 1687. He amassed a large fortune and was a leader in the political arena, protesting for recognition of the Dissenters and their religious freedoms. He was one of the sixty-three petitioners granted the rights and privileges of citizenship by an Act of Assembly dated March 10, 1696, and in 1716 he was one of the petitioners to the Crown against the Proprietors. He was quite active in church duties; his signature appears on a call for a pastor for the church in 1724. Church records also show his name among subscribers for a new church building in 1729 and on a list of pew holders in 1734. He died at age seventy-six, having acquired, according to the *South Carolina Gazette*, "a large Fortune" and "a fair Character." He and his wife Desiré had at least seven children. Four of their children and eleven of their grandchildren are buried in the churchyard.

The grave of their granddaughter, Martha Peronneau, who died at the age of thirteen in 1746, is one of the more appealing graves in the churchyard. It "shows a soul effigy with a cheeky, youthful looking face, a

Sarah Freer, 1760. *Courtesy Natalie Simpson* (C).

lifelike mouth, a nose with well-defined nostrils, finely detailed hair and a big dimple in the chin. The lines around the figure's eyes draw attention to a hopeful gaze, and the scallop shells carved atop the stone's side panels are a symbol of new life and the resurrection."[17] The Peronneaus share a plot in the graveyard with the Vanderhorsts, their relatives, who were also prominent Huguenot merchants and planters.

One of the most unique gravestones in the churchyard is that of Mary Owen. She is one of the few women of the period mentioned for anything other than being a wife and mother. She was a milliner in a time when few women had businesses. The stone shows a smiling face, which was unusual during this period, and is the only known grave portrait to have a hat (probably because of her profession). On the stone, she is also wearing a string of pearls. Her father, Thomas Corker, and her husband, Richard Owen, are referred to as "gent." (meaning gentleman) on her tombstone, which indicated an aristocrat who had gained his wealth through a profession. The stone tells us that her father was from "Shavington Com Greastie in the County of Chester." It was a colonial-era tradition to include the names of a woman's parents and husband on the tombstone.[18]

Born in 1691 in New York, Lucas Stoutenburgh was a prominent Independent Meeting House member of Dutch ancestry. By 1717 he was in Charleston and was one of many signers of an address to the king explaining South Carolina's Indian troubles and praying for relief from high taxes caused by defense needs.[19] In 1721, he was a captain of one of the militia companies and in June of that year was in "Command of ye Watch in Charlestown." He was a silversmith and one of his spoons is on display today in the Charleston Museum; another is on display at the Museum of Early Southern Decorative Arts in Winston-Salem, North Carolina.[20]

Henry Peronneau Sr., 1743. *Courtesy Missy Loewe* (A1).

Peronneau and Vanderhorst graves. *Courtesy Natalie Simpson* (A1).

Martha Peronneau, 1746. *Courtesy Missy Loewe* (A1).

Desiré Peronneau, 1740. *Courtesy Daniel Farber* (A1).

Christopher Peronneau, 1743. Note tree roots bulging between stones. *Courtesy Daniel Farber* (A1).

Eleazer Phillips was, his gravestone states, "His Majesty's first Printer for ye province of South Carolina." He was "Born in Boston in N. England…He departed this Life July 10th 1732. Aged 21 Years & 10 Mo." While the cause of Mr. Phillips's death is not specified, July 1732 marked the beginning of one of Charleston's worst epidemics of yellow fever, which killed 133 whites and "a great many slaves, amounting to about 7 percent of the city's population, before it subsided in September."[21]

Charleston real estate investment was profitable then as now. Early real estate records show that Ebenezer Simmons, a Charleston merchant and member of the Independent Meeting House, received a transfer of property for land on which the Old Exchange and Provost Dungeon was later built. For a while the land was rented for one peppercorn until the final sale, in 1738, at which time the exchange took place for "£800 current money." In 1767, appraisers of the land paid him £5,500 for the same property.[22]

The leadership of the church in 1724 is documented in the forty-three names listed on pages 25–26. Many of the names can be seen today throughout Charleston on its street signs and in its history books. Their descendants bear them proudly. Their signatures are on a letter issuing a call to the Rev. Nathan Basset to become pastor of the congregation. The call is recorded in the earliest currently existing register of the church. The formal fashion and the terms of the letter are of interest.

Mary Owen, 1749. *Courtesy Missy Loewe* (B).

In the name of our Lord and Saviour Jesus Christ: Amen.

We the members of the Presbyterian Church in Charlestown, and others resorting to this Public Place of Worship…being very satisfied of your ability and Capacity to take upon you the Pastoral Charge of Us…do humbly beseech and invite you, the Re'd Nathan Bassett, to accept and take you the Office and Charge of a Minister or Pastor over us, to administer unto Us God's Holy word and Ordinances; and to do whatever else appertain or anyways belong to a Minister of the Gospel. And on our part we do Solemnly promise and declare in the presence of God and this Congregation that We will at all Time endeavor to behave and carry ourselves towards You, as becomes Christians to do towards a Minister of Jesus Christ; and as you will dispense unto Us your spiritual things, so We shall not be wanting constantly to administer unto you of our Temporal. Humbly desiring that you'l please to accept of this our call and invitation.

Luke Stoutenburgh	*John Carmichael*	*John Fraser*	*John Ballentine*
John Ellis	*Joseph Massey*	*Joseph Bany*	*Samuel Morris*
Daniel Townsend	*Henry Varnor*	*William Scott*	*Moses Plummer*
John Jeffords	*Stephen Bedon*	*Robert Fladger*	*John Bohannan*

Above left: Eleazer Phillips, 1732. *Courtesy Natalie Simpson* (B).

Above right: The grave of Nathan Bassett, 1738. This is the oldest portrait stone in America. Note the holes in the stone; it was removed from the wall of the church when the accessibility ramp was installed. *Courtesy Missy Loewe* (A2).

Thomas Barksdale	John Millins	Benjamin Jones	Robert Bohannan
Thomas Holton	John Simmons	Samuel Eveleigh	Garrett Van Velsen
Henry Peronneau*	Solomon Legare*	Timothy Bellamy	Francis Holmes, Junr
Ebenezer Simmons	Anthony Mathewes, Junr	John Milner	Benjamin Massey
Henry Saltus	James Ballantine	James Mathewes*	Dun Campbell
Joseph Moody	Anthony Mathewes (Sr.)*	Miles Brewton	Edgar Wells
Jeremiah Milner*	George Ducat	Nathaniel Mariner	

*Tombstones of the persons whose names are starred can be seen in the churchyard to this day.

BUILDINGS AND PROPERTY

Gradually, as population and fortunes grew, early church property was expanded through gifts of the congregation. In 1707 a bequest from Frances Simons of her plot of garden ground lying east of (and adjoining) the church lot extended the property toward what is now St. Philip's churchyard. Other land was donated to form the plot that is now the graveyard, and still other lots near what is now the Unitarian Church on Archdale were given.[23]

The first building lasted about fifty years. A call for subscriptions for a new building went out to the congregation at the end of 1729. This call documents the prosperity and commerce that were Charleston's at the time. It reads:

> *Whereas the present publick meeting house in Charles Towne, which in the early times, or beginning of the settlement thereof, was erected and built for the publick worship of God after the Presbyterian form and discipline, is now by long time gone to decay and becoming very old and out of repair: And whereas by God's blessing not only the inhabitants of the said town are increased, but by means of the vast growth of our trade, a great number of sea-faring and transient persons come to and frequent this port, so that the said Meeting House is also found to be too small and inconvenient to receive and contain the whole number of people which repair thither for worship.*[24]

The names of Colonel Miles Brewton, Robert Tradd, George Ducat, Joseph Moody and Thomas Lamboll were proposed as being "Persons fit and proper to be intrusted with the said Work" of enlarging, rebuilding and accommodating the meetinghouse. Progress was swift. A total of 104 persons donated from 1.10 shillings to £100, amounting to £8,322.15. In 1731, an additional £332 were given to enlarge the building twenty-two feet, and a base was added for the steeple. It contained forty-seven pews that were subject to an annual assessment.[25] By 1732 the new building was ready for occupancy and pews were assigned.

2.

SECOND CHURCH BUILDING, 1732 TO 1804

This period of Circular's history is as remarkable as that of the first era. During these years the courage and conviction of its congregation were tested by plague, fire and war. The original meetinghouse was replaced and a second meetinghouse, on Archdale Street, was added at the dawn of the Revolution to accommodate a growing congregation. The church, still called the Independent Meeting House, was to have a strong influence on the events of its time. Its leaders were among the most important political figures of the Revolution and some of the wealthiest men in the colonies.

The new brick building on Meeting Street, sometimes called the "Brick Meeting House" during its first few years, was ready by November 1732, just shy of three years after the call went out for subscriptions to fund it. The new building was of oblong shape, forty feet by sixty-two and a half feet, with a tower added at the front or west end.[26] There were forty-seven pews besides the minister's and one other large pew for strangers. Additionally, there was a gallery at the west end with benches adjoining the belfry. Indications are that the door was on the south side of the church. Pews were assessed annually and were assigned to subscribers according to their respective claims as contributors. Samuel Fley was given pew number one in the first year. The church register contains a list of forty-five pew holders for forty-seven pews; thus, not many pews were unoccupied when the church opened.[27]

A clerk was appointed by the minister, for "Ringing the Bell, taking Care of and keeping Clean said Meeting-House, Pews and Seats, and for Weeding the Yard, etc." The clerk also had the "Priviledge of digging all Graves to be made in the Ground belonging to said Meeting-House," for which he was to be paid "Twenty shillings for each Grave…one half thereof for his own proper Use," the other half to be used for repairing the fences.[28]

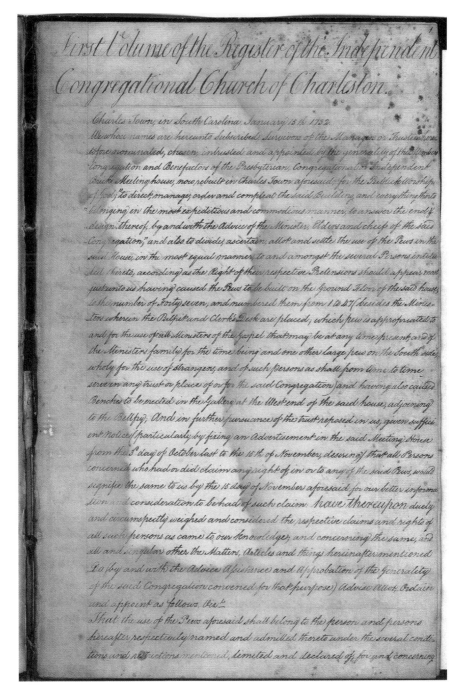

First Register of the Independent Congregational Church of Charleston, 1732. *Courtesy South Carolina Historical Society.*

Rev. James Parker, 1742, pastor of Independent Meeting House from 1740 to 1742. *Courtesy Natalie Simpson* (A2).

In 1734 the Rev. Josiah Smith was called to co-pastor with Rev. Nathan Bassett. In 1738, after Rev. Nathan Bassett's death, the church sent a letter to London that described what the congregation was looking for in its minister. They desired someone "learned, bright and popular." He was to have a "strong, audible voice, clear and distinct pronunciation, good elocution and decent deportment of body in the pulpit." He should be "affable in temper and conversation and have great moderation in principles." They wanted a "gentleman (if obtainable) who has an agreeable address in his preaching and conversation, solid judgment and an affable temper." The compensation offered was £100 sterling per year, use of the house and grounds as parsonage and "the use of the negro." They also offered to pay all travel expenses from England, as well as all travel expenses back there if there was dissatisfaction on either side after a year.[29] Rev. James Parker answered the call, but died after only two years.

The First (Scots) Presbyterian Church held its first service in its new house of worship on Meeting Street south of Tradd in 1734. This church was founded by twelve Scots families who left the Independent Meeting House to establish a church with stricter Presbyterian government and doctrine. They also desired to have only Scottish ministers.[30] The church, called First (Scots), provided the most numerous group of Loyalists during the Revolution. This would be one of several churches whose members left the

First (Scots) Presbyterian Church at 53 Meeting Street, built in 1814, founded in 1734.

French Huguenot Church at 140 Meeting Street, 1845. *Both photographs courtesy Paul Calhoun.*

original Dissenter church. Some Huguenot members of the Independent Meeting House left to join the Huguenot Church built in 1687. The current French Huguenot Church on Church Street was built in 1845.

Church records show that many Presbyterians and French Huguenots remained at the Independent or Brick Meeting House, preferring the truly independent policy of this church that "was not so much to define exactly the particular mode of their discipline, and to bind their hands up to any other stiff form adopted either by Presbyterians, Congregationalists or Independents, as to be upon a broad dissenting bottom and to leave ourselves as free as possible from any foreign shackles, that no moderate persons of either denominations might be afraid to join them."[31]

Addition of silver to the church inventory documents the continuing prosperity of the church during this period. Members agreed in 1754 that a subscription paper be prepared and sent about to enable the deacons of the church to purchase "Silver-Plate for the Administration of the Blessed Sacrament of the Lord's Supper."[32] Within a few years, the following silver items were purchased:

Two hand-hammered tankards of plain design, fluted in delicate arched fashion. One is attributed to Samuel Wells, 1751–52 of London, England; the other to Thomas Whipham, 1756–57, London.

Two large sterling wafer trays (communion plates) with plain flange. Church inventory of 1963 attributes them to William Gurley (1804) of Norwich, Connecticut; however, more recent research attributes them to William Gowdey of Charleston, South Carolina, 1757. This date is more in line with dates of the tankards.[33]

Silver from this period in Charleston's history is extremely rare, and Circular is fortunate to own these today. Church records show that as membership grew, the church felt they needed additional communion pieces. As treasurer, Josiah Smith Jr. asked Enos Reeves, a local silversmith, to make one large and two smaller wine cups with handles & shifting covers for sacramental use in 1799. All of these pieces are on loan to the Charleston Museum.

In 1753, Rev. James Edmonds, who had preached in Cainhoy, South Carolina, was engaged as a lecturer for six months when there was no response to a letter sent to London following the resignation of Rev. Josiah Smith in 1750. Not until 1757 was the Rev. William Hutson called to join Rev. James Edmonds as a full-time co-pastor at the Independent Church.

Circular Congregational Church antique silver. *Courtesy Mary Jane Ogawa.*

Hutson's career had an interesting beginning. In 1740 he was a young man in New York, newly arrived from London, escaping family pressures and an unwanted career in law to try his hand at acting. He went to hear the noted evangelist Rev. George Whitefield preach and was so moved by what he heard that he changed careers and decided to devote himself to God.

With Rev. Whitefield's help, Hutson moved to the Beaufort, South Carolina area and by 1743 had his own church, the Stoney Creek Independent Presbyterian Church. He married Mary Woodward Chardon, granddaughter of Rev. Henry Woodward, the first English settler in South Carolina. After thirteen years at Stoney Creek, the Hutsons and their six children moved to Charleston in 1756. Mary Hutson passed away in 1757. Hutson remarried but soon lost his second wife as well. He had two sons and four daughters; one daughter became the wife of Colonel Isaac Hayne, who was hanged in 1781 by the British. Rev. Hutson died in 1761 and is buried between his two wives in Circular's cemetery. His son, Richard, was imprisoned by the British during the Revolutionary War, was a delegate to

Rev. William Hutson.
Portrait by Jeremiah Theus

Mrs. William Hutson.
Portrait by Jeremiah Theus.
*Both images courtesy South
Carolina Historical Society.*

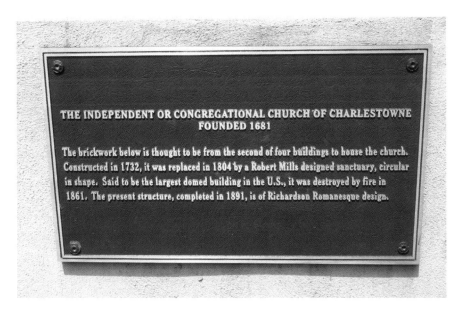

Plaque explaining old foundation bricks from 1759. *Courtesy Natalie Simpson* (A2).

the Continental Congress, signed the Articles of Confederation and was the first intendant (mayor) of Charleston. His James Earle portrait is hanging in Charleston City Hall.

In 1759 the members and supporters of the church felt that an addition to the building was needed, as there was not a single vacant pew, and many persons had made application for pews that could not be granted. They decided to add on to the east end so that a certain pillar at pew fifteen would become the center of the church. As the church was forty feet wide and was extended to the rear, there is little doubt that the brick foundation now plainly visible above the ground at the rear of the present church is the old foundation of the 1759 addition. It is just forty feet wide and ninety feet from the front, thus making the enlarged church ninety feet long.[34] There is a plaque on the accessibility ramp wall explaining the 1759 brick foundation visible above ground.

After the death of Rev. Hutson in 1761, Rev. Edmonds continued as pastor until 1767. He remained in Charleston and was exiled, with other members of the congregation, to Philadelphia during the Revolution. In 1761, Rev. Andrew Bennett, who was a native of London, came to Charleston from a church in Philadelphia to become co-pastor here. He left Charleston after a year because of ill health.

Rev. John Thomas, a native of Wales, came to Charleston in 1767 as a young man to become pastor after Rev. Bennett's departure. Rev. Thomas

Thomas Lamboll Thomas, 1770, son of Rev. John Thomas and Mary Lamboll Thomas, who died at the age of one year. *Courtesy Circular Church Graveyard Records (CCGR)* (B).

died of consumption at the age of twenty-six because of his devotion to the salvation and care of a man condemned to death for a crime. After the man's execution, Thomas had the body transferred to James Island on a cold March night, where he performed the funeral service at the grave at 10:00 p.m. in order to save the body from dissection. He caught a violent cold, which rapidly led to consumption and resulted in his death the following summer. In spite of his short life, he married the daughter of Thomas Lamboll and fathered three children: a son who died in infancy and two girls.

ISSUES OF SLAVERY

Records of this period, however scarce, indicate that members of the Independent Meeting House owned slaves. There is also evidence that the congregation had lost none of its independent, Dissenter spirit and its openness to all ideas, revealing the dichotomy under which these members lived. From its beginning in the colony, slavery presented Dissenters with the dilemma of trying to reconcile their commercial needs with their love of freedom and their Christian ethic. Led by Rev. Josiah Smith, the Independent Meeting House congregation invited the controversial Rev. George Whitefield, the great revivalist, to preach. In his sermon he warned

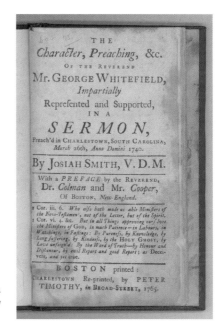

Rev. George Whitefield's sermon, from a pamphlet by Josiah Smith. *Courtesy University South Carolina, Caroliniana Library*.

the people of Charleston that the Stono Rebellion, a slave insurrection put down only a few months before, was a divine judgment on them for their sins. Whitefield, who became a founder of the movement in the colonies called the Great Awakening, appealed to Southern masters to support "the evangelization of the slaves." When he returned to Charleston in 1740, he again preached at the Independent Meeting House. Whitefield was denied the opportunity to preach in Anglican churches in Charleston because of his perceived radicalism.[35] The official Church of England in the colony was opposed to his crusade to evangelize the slaves. If successful, evangelization would have nullified one of the justifications for slavery at the time—that the slaves were not Christian.

The same George Whitefield and Rev. Josiah Smith, minister at the Independent Meeting House, were influential in the history of American slavery by their roles in the events that led John Newton to write the great hymn "Amazing Grace" and become a minister. While in Charleston, Newton, who was an officer on a slave ship, was favorably impressed by a sermon preached at the Independent church by Rev. Josiah Smith. Newton prayed and was able to "taste the sweets of communion." Back in England, he was moved to repent by the preaching of George Whitefield and later wrote his famous hymn. He was persuaded by John Wesley and Whitefield to enter the Anglican ministry. As a minister, he convinced the young William Wilberforce, in the crisis of his conversion, to remain in Parliament.

While in Parliament, Wilberforce championed the antislavery cause.[36] Thus, a sermon by Josiah Smith at the Independent Meeting House eventually had international ramifications in the slavery debate.

Not much is known about the African American members of our church during the time prior to the Revolutionary War, as church records do not include exact numbers, but they do give some indications. In 1772, complaints surfaced about the number of black people sitting in the aisles. A committee assigned to "make provision for accommodating the black people with seats in some suitable part of the Church reported shortly thereafter that there would be seating available for forty or fifty Blacks at the North and East wall benches."[37] In 1804, when the church was planning a new building, a committee decided that "the North side of the gallery be appropriated for the accommodation of such people of color who worship in the Church."[38] The earliest references in the church records, while they offer no official membership numbers, reveal that a significant number of blacks attended the Circular Church during the late colonial period.[39] The first book of records still in existence lists among the marriages, births and deaths from 1732 to 1738 the following:

> *Abraham, a negro man of Mr. Samuel Jones' was baptized Aug. the 11th, 1734 by me,* (signed) *Nathan Bassett.*
> *Peter, an adult negro man was baptized 30th December, 1737 by me,* (signed) *Nathan Bassett.*
> *Mary and Susannah her daughter, negroes of Landgrave Thomas Smith were baptized the 7th of April 1738 by me, Nathan Bassett.*[40]

There are no further baptismal entries, white or black, until 1784, when they appear in another book, with occasional entries like the above interspersed with white baptisms until 1790, at which time they are separated. Only once does the word "slave" appear. Usually it is "servant" or "belonging to." There are two cases where African American children are baptized and then said to be adopted by the master or mistress. It is thought that this was done so that the child could be taught to read. Occasionally one is baptized as a "free-man, formerly a servant."[41]

In church baptismal records from 1784 to 1815, 417 people are identified as either "servant," "black," "negro," "free person" or "slave." The names of their owners and former owners are given. For example: "Lordsday July 26, 1801 Baptized Abram, a free man formerly a servant of Mrs. Williamson, & Sapho, his wife belonging to Dr. R. Wilson."[42]

Slavery is also documented on gravestones during this period. The Rev. William Hutson is described in his epitaph as a "kind master," indicating

Samuel Jones, 1755, slave owner. *Courtesy Paul Calhoun* (B).

that he owned slaves. In 1751 he records the baptism of "Pricilla & her two children Alsey & Nanny, slaves belonging to me myself," and another baptism recorded on April 20, 1755, of "Jacob, a young Negro of my own, Son of Jacob & Lissey."[43] Six other graves were located that are marked with comments like "kind," "indulgent" or "humane" master, dating from 1768 to 1828. Besides Rev. Hutson, there are Dr. Richard Savage, William Dandridge, Thomas Legare, John Ashe, a relative of Anthony Toomer and Captain John Mercier. Mercier's epitaph was typical of those that mentioned being slave owners. It tells us that "He was an affectionate Husband, a humane Master and sincere Friend." Mr. William Dandridge's stone likewise praises him as a "tender and loving Husband, a kind Relative, a good Master."

Revolutionary ideology embracing freedom and independence was for whites only, not for slaves. When Dr. David Ramsay, the noted historian, came to Charleston in 1774 from Philadelphia and joined the Independent Church, he was critical of slavery. However, by 1778, Ramsay wrote of the slaves, "We cannot do without them. Our lands cannot be cultivated by white men." White prosperity and freedom depended upon black slavery. "Freedom for whites appeared to demand slavery for blacks."[44] Ramsay himself owned a few slaves, and was married to Martha Laurens Ramsay,

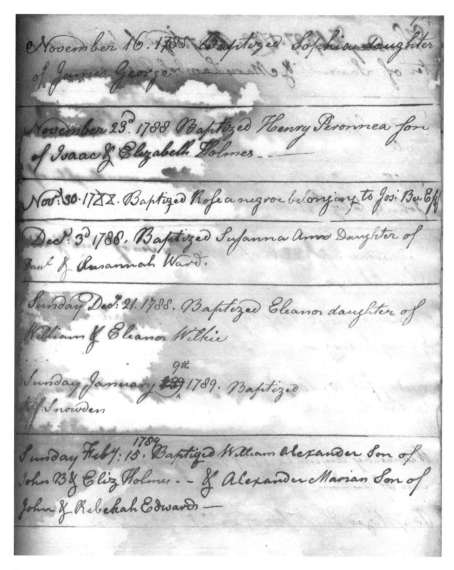

Page from Circular Church baptismal records listing free and enslaved people, beginning with 1792. *Courtesy South Carolina Historical Society.*

Mr. William Dandridge, 1768. *Courtesy CCGR* (B).

who was the daughter of Henry Laurens. Laurens shows the struggle of the wealthy planter and merchant who was wrestling with the morality of his actions.

Henry Laurens was one of the major slave traders in the United States; he may also have been the richest man. Henry's son, John (Martha's brother), studied in England and became opposed to slavery. He urged his father in letters to free all of his slaves. Henry agreed that it was the moral thing to do, but argued that to do so would deprive his children, including John, of their inheritance. Later, Laurens would become president of the Continental Congress, which was the equivalent of being the president of the United States today. At his son John's urging, he proposed to the Congress that slaves be given their freedom if they fought against the British. The proposal was defeated.

Most church members owned slaves; some were deeply involved in the slave trade. Between 1735 and 1749, three members alone—Benjamin Savage, Paul Jenys and William Cleland—imported 42 percent of all slave cargoes in South Carolina.[45] The fact that members of the Independent Meeting House were slave owners was crucial to the way they viewed the world and to decisions they made when involved in setting up the new country's political and economic systems.

MEMBERS OF NOTE

The people of this second church building era were some of the strongest and most interesting in the history of the church. The lives of these men and women helped determine the fate of our country. They risked everything for a war of independence, built a country and their personal fortunes, endured losing their families to the plagues rampant in Charleston and went into exile rather than betray their Dissenter instincts. Though their circumstances varied from blue collar to aristocrat, they had in common the courage of their convictions and the will to survive and flourish.

One of the most interesting and famous of Charleston's Patriots was David Ramsay, mentioned in the previous section as the son-in-law of Henry Laurens. Ramsay was a physician, born in Pennsylvania in 1749, the son of a poor, Irish immigrant farmer, James Ramsay. His father was determined that his sons would achieve higher positions in life and sent all three to Princeton College. David Ramsay was so gifted that he had read the entire Bible by the time he was six, and had memorized a good portion of it. He took the examination to enter Princeton, was admitted as a junior and graduated at the age of sixteen. He studied physics and got a medical degree from the College of Pennsylvania in Philadelphia in 1773. After practicing medicine for a year, he decided to move to Charleston.

Ramsay was a staunch Presbyterian and became a member of the Independent Meeting House. His first wife, Sabina Ellis, a descendant of early church member Solomon Legare, died after a few months of their marriage. Ramsay was active in state politics and was a strong supporter of independence. He served briefly in the army as a surgeon. Because of his patriotic activities, he was exiled to St. Augustine, Florida, by the British in 1780 and then to Philadelphia, where he married his second wife, who died five days after giving birth to their son, John. In 1782 Ramsay was elected to the Confederation Congress, and was later elected its president. In 1789 he wrote a groundbreaking work, *The History of the American Revolution*. Ramsay ran for the United States House and then for the United States Senate, but lost both races, probably because of his liberal views on slavery. He did serve in the South Carolina State Legislature, including six years as president of the Senate. Dr. Ramsay was one of several South Carolina physicians who promoted the use of vaccination against smallpox.[46]

Dr. Ramsay's third wife, Martha, became one of the more well-known women of her time. Interesting stories about her abound. Her father, Henry Laurens, was the first person in America to be cremated. As the story goes, Martha almost died of smallpox when she was a baby. She was thought to be dead and was laid out near a window for her funeral. The fresh air

David Ramsay, 1815, and other family members. His name does not show, as it has been broken off. *Courtesy Natalie Simpson* (B).

Portrait of Doctor David Ramsay, circa 1796, attributed to Rembrandt Peale (American, 1778–1860), oil on canvas. *Courtesy Gibbes Museum of Art/ Carolina Art Association, XX1914.*

apparently revived her, and she was saved from being buried alive. As a result of this incident her father developed a phobia about being buried alive, and so chose cremation. She was probably the intellectual equal of her husband, Dr. Ramsay, as she could read fluently by age three, and could supposedly do so in an inverted position without any difficulty. Ramsay credited her with the idea of a circular design for the new church building in 1806. A deeply religious person, she was educated in Europe and bore Dr. Ramsay eleven children in sixteen years.

Her friend, Catherine Futerell, lived with them for years and probably helped in caring for the children. Ms. Futerell was the daughter of a jailor in the Tower of London when Henry Laurens was imprisoned there for fifteen months, until he was exchanged for Lord Cornwallis. She and Martha became friends then, and she came with the family when they returned to America. One of the Ramsays' daughters was named for Ms. Futerell.

Another woman of unusual prominence for that time period was Elizabeth Lamboll, the wife of Thomas Lamboll, the young man who described the hurricane of 1713. He was clerk of the church for more than forty years and was also a prominent judge. Elizabeth, who was thirty years his junior, was a noted horticulturist. Through the sharing of seeds and root stock as well as cultivation techniques, she helped people throughout South Carolina establish gardens. Judge Lamboll was drawn into her gardening interests and began to catalogue her stock and document her methods. He corresponded with John Bartram, a naturalist from Philadelphia, sharing Elizabeth's techniques, samples of her plants and root stocks. Partly because of her help, Bartram eventually became the foremost naturalist in the colonies and was named botanist to the queen.

Nathaniel Russell was one of the most notable members of the Independent Church. He was known as the "King of the Yankees" because of his success and because he helped to found the New England Society just before his death. His ancestors had been leaders of thought and action in New England for 150 years. His father, Joseph Russell, was chief justice of Rhode Island.[47]

When Russell first came to Charleston, he built a wharf and a warehouse on the Bay and had an office and residence across the street from them. He conducted business on the lower floor and had living quarters above. From this modest beginning he became one of the wealthiest men in the United States. Because he was "in trade," however, he was considered of inferior standing by the more socially acceptable planters, doctors, lawyers and clergymen of the Lowcountry aristocracy. According to legend, he built his house as a showplace for his two marriageable daughters. At 51 Meeting Street, it was located in a neighborhood that was just becoming

Above: Elizabeth Lamboll, 1770. *Courtesy Natalie Simpson* (B).

Right: Nathaniel Russell House, 51 Meeting Street. *Courtesy Paul Calhoun.*

Nathaniel Russell, 1820.
Courtesy Natalie Simpson (C).

a residential area for the more affluent people of Charleston. Today it is operated as a museum by the Historic Charleston Foundation. His tomb in Circular graveyard is an eight-foot-tall, four-sided, very impressive, marble monument reflective of his wealth.

The Honorable Isaac Holmes presents another interesting story of how men of this period settled here and rose to power. Holmes came from Boston, where his father was a merchant and tavern operator. He sent his son, Isaac, to Charleston to see to his landholdings in South Carolina. Isaac became a successful merchant and ship captain. He married Henry Peronneau's daughter, which helped cement his success, as the Peronneaus were very wealthy. Holmes served in a variety of civic positions and helped found the South Carolina Library Society, one of America's first subscription libraries. He also was a founder of the Friendly Society for the Mutual Insurance of Houses Against Fires, one of the first insurance companies in America.[48]

The plaque on Josiah Flagg's monument tells of America's first dentist who served in the American Revolution and the War of 1812.

Isaac Holmes, 1751, carved by H. Emmes of Boston. It is unusual in that it has a portrait and a skull and crossbones. *Courtesy Missy Loewe* (B).

Plaque in memory of Josiah Flagg, 1816. *Courtesy Natalie Simpson* (B).

One of the saddest and most frightening aspects of life in colonial Charleston must have been the frequent epidemics of malaria, yellow fever and smallpox that killed so many. Wealth was no protection against these deaths. The story of the Savage family is a good example of how many families were decimated. Dr. Richard Savage and his wife Mary lost three boys who died within ten days of one another in August of 1784: John Clifford, age seven; William, age three; and Dandridge, age five. They are buried together in one crypt. The inscription is a heart-wrenching show of grief:

Exposed to Worms lies three once charming Boys
The Father's Comfort and the Mother's Joy
These Youths at once fair Fruit and Blossoms bore
Much in Possession in Expectance more
T'wou'd grieve you tender Reader to relate
The hasty strides of unrelenting fate
Direfull decree all human Art was vain
The Power of Med'cine faill'd the healing train
But happy Youths by Death made truly great
Had Life been lengthen'd to its utmost date
What had they known but Sorrow, Pain and Woe
The Curse entailed on Adam's Race below
They're only safe who thru Death's Gates have Pas'd
And reached that evermore will last
How vain is Man, how fluttering are his Joys,
When what one Moment gives, the next destroys
Hope and Despair fill up his round of Life
And all his Joys are one continual Strife.

As if losing these three children was not hard enough, near their crypt in the churchyard are the graves of their two brothers who died three years later, less than one month apart: Richard, age four, and Clifford, age three. The fact that they died within a month of one another suggests they probably died of the same illness.

REVOLUTIONARY WAR PERIOD

Shaped by its independent mind and goaded by a colonial government that treated Dissenters with contempt, this church became fertile ground for revolutionary sentiment in the colony. Prominent members of this

Above: Savage crypt, 1784. *Courtesy Natalie Simpson* (B).

Right: Richard Savage, 1787. *Courtesy CCGR* (B).

Clifford Savage, 1788. *Courtesy CCGR* (B).

second meetinghouse, and its distinguished minister, Rev. William Tennent, frequently spoke out for political and religious freedom.

Tennent, who was only thirty-two when he was called as minister to the Independent Meeting House, was elected to the Provincial Congress that met in 1775. He was an ardent advocate both of the independence of the Dissenting churches from the Church of England and of the colonies from the Crown of England.[49] Tennent gave his talents wholeheartedly to the cause of the Patriots. He wrote newspaper articles praising independence, and when it was necessary for the assembly to meet on Sundays, he was "occasionally heard both in his church and in the State-House, addressing different audiences with equal animation on their spiritual and temporal interests."[50]

In 1775, the Provincial Congress of South Carolina sent William Tennent, noted politician William Henry Drayton and Oliver Hart, who was the minister of the Baptist church in Charleston, to make a tour of the backcountry to inform the people there of the current events and to attempt to enlist their support in the fight for independence. The journey was rigorous and, at times, discouraging; however, the successful mission contributed to the struggle for independence in South Carolina.[51]

Upon his return to Charleston, Tennent gave unsparingly of his time to Congressional deliberations. He drew up a petition in favor of liberty, which united the different denominations of Dissenters in its support, and procured several thousand signatures.[52] When the constitution for the new state was being considered in 1777, he made an impassioned speech on behalf of religious toleration. He urged, "Let us bury what is past forever…Let it be a foundation article in your constitution. That there shall be no establishment of one religious denomination of Christians in preference to another. That none shall be obliged to pay to the support of worship in which they do not freely join." Tennent was successful in his endeavor, and after the adoption of the constitution of 1790 there was no longer an established church in South Carolina.

As busy as he was with politics, he was also mindful of his Independent Meeting House in Charleston. He proposed that they build a second church, on Archdale Street, and raised enough money to see to it. Tennent served as a chaplain for a short while in the Continental army, but died of fever at the early age of thirty-seven, shortly after the Revolution began. The Independent Church erected a monument to his memory in their house of worship on Archdale Street, where it may still be seen in the vestibule of what is now the Unitarian Church of Charleston.[53]

A noteworthy result of Tennent's proposal to build a second church was that a committee was appointed in 1778 to revise the constitution of the church with particular reference to the dual arrangements necessary because of the two houses of worship. The seven men appointed were John Edwards, Josiah Smith Jr., Dr. David Ramsay, Richard Hutson, Thomas Legare Jr., James Thomson and Edward Darrell. Despite the fact that they were in the middle of war these men documented their dedication to their church by taking the time and effort to write the necessary new constitution. The language of the document, especially Article 10, also reveals their independent spirit in religious matters as well as political:

> *Article 10. In matters of Church Government we hold it to be our unalienable right as a Christian Church to govern ourselves in that which appears most expedient to our own members and most suitable to our circumstances without control in Ecclesiastical Matters from any Man or set of Men, nevertheless we think it prudent to ask advice of such Protestant Dissenting Church and Ministers as to us seems proper.*[54]

As Tennent was agitating in favor of freedom of religion, another group of Patriots, the Sons of Liberty, began meeting under the "Liberty Tree" in Charleston in 1766. Sons of Liberty groups were organized throughout the colonies to protest the Stamp Act, despite the attempts of the British to eradicate them.[55] These artisans, or mechanics, of Charleston have been called the "prime movers" in opposing Great Britain during the early years

NEAR THIS SPOT
ONCE STOOD
THE LIBERTY TREE
WHERE COLONIAL INDEPENDENCE
WAS FIRST ADVOCATED BY
CHRISTOPHER GADSDEN
A.D. 1766
AND WHERE TEN YEARS LATER
THE DECLARATION OF
INDEPENDENCE
WAS FIRST HEARD
AND APPLAUDED BY
SOUTH CAROLINIANS

ERECTED BY THE LOCAL SOCIETY OF
THE SONS OF THE REVOLUTION
A.D. 1903

Plaque on Alexander Street just north of Calhoun Street, commemorating the "Liberty Tree," where the Sons of Liberty met. *Courtesy Pat Spaulding.*

of the Revolutionary cause. They held public meetings at "a most noble live oak tree in Mr. Mazyck's pasture," which they formally dedicated to Liberty, thereafter called the Liberty Tree.[56] A plaque commemorates the spot near what is now the corner of Alexander and Calhoun Streets.

Some radicals who would not subscribe to the oath of allegiance were jailed aboard two British prison ships lying in the harbor. The list of prisoners on these ships almost repeats the roll of a meeting at Liberty Tree. While most members of the Sons of Liberty were artisans and mechanics, the members from the Independent Meeting House included wealthy members of the planter, merchant and political class as well. While they were incarcerated, smallpox broke out; death carts passed daily from the ships to the graveyards.[57]

The following regulars of the Independent Meeting House were Sons of Liberty. Half of them signed the 1778 church constitution and nearly all are buried in the graveyard:

ANTHONY TOOMER—builder and brick mason (he laid bricks for the Charleston Orphan House)*

JOB PALMER—carpenter (four of his grandsons later became ministers, one at the Independent Church)+

RICHARD YEADON—clock and watchmaker (his grandson became a newspaper editor) P

THOMAS YOU—silversmith and goldsmith P

BENJAMIN HAWES—gilder, painter and coach maker

DAVID RAMSAY—physician and historian*

JOHN FULLERTON—carpenter

THOMAS DOUGHTY—carpenter

JOSIAH SMITH JR.—extremely wealthy merchant, son of Rev. Josiah Smith*

JOHN EDWARDS—wealthy merchant (died in exile in Philadelphia)*

RICHARD HUTSON—first intendant (mayor), son of Rev. William Hutson *

* indicates exile to St. Augustine and to Philadelphia
+ indicates exile to Philadelphia
P indicates imprisonment on a prison ship

In 1778, in confirmation with the independence displayed from its beginning, the Independent Congregational Meeting House loaned its funds, amounting to £18,757, to the state treasury in support of the Revolution.[58] Individual members of the Independent Church also contributed large parts of their fortunes to South Carolina's resistance during the Revolutionary War. Several members of the church made large loans to the state

HEREIN LIE THE REMAINS OF

RICHARD HUTSON
1747~1795

SON OF REV. WILLIAM AND MARY WOODWARD HUTSON
SOUTH CAROLINA PATRIOT, STATESMAN AND JURIST
GRADUATED PRINCETON 1765
FOUNDING BODY THE COLLEGE OF CHARLESTON
1772~1794
MEMBER S.C. GENERAL ASSEMBLY
AND LEGISLATIVE COUNCIL 1776~1790
SERVED IN MILITIA AND IMPRISONED
BY THE BRITISH
DURING THE REVOLUTIONARY WAR
DELEGATE TO CONTINENTAL CONGRESS 1778~1779
SIGNER ARTICLES OF CONFEDERATION
LIEUTENANT GOVERNOR 1782~1783
AUTHOR OF ACT INCORPORATING
CITY OF CHARLESTON 1783
FIRST INTENDANT (MAYOR) OF CHARLESTON 1783
JUDGE COURT OF CHANCERY 1784~1794
SENIOR JUDGE 1791~1794

Plaque commemorating Richard Hutson. *Courtesy Natalie Simpson* (C).

Right: Hon. John Edwards, 1781 family tomb. (C).

Below: Anthony Toomer, 1798. *Both photographs courtesy CCGR* (B).

Hon. John Edwards House, 15 Meeting Street. *Courtesy Paul Calhoun.*

government during the war. John Edwards made the largest loan of any of the states' bondholders (£400,000), and Josiah Smith Jr. was the second largest bondholder through his own personal funds and a number of others that he controlled, lending £100,000.[59]

John Milner, a prominent gunsmith and church member, was among those imprisoned in the Provost Dungeon after the British captured the city of Charleston in 1780. Martha Milner, his teenage daughter, smuggled boiled rice, which she carried in her pockets, to her father and fed him through the iron bars or grating. Many years later, after her death at age ninety, Martha's grandson erected a marker over her grave in Circular churchyard, the inscription of which honored her heroism when she was fourteen years old: "She was herself a witness and heroic sufferer bearing to her grave the scar of a wound received in a bayonet thrust when only 14 years old while defending her child-brother from the violence of a Tory."[60]

When the British seized the city in 1780, eighty men were sent as prisoners of war to St. Augustine, Florida. Of these, about half were members of the Independent Church. Many of them had already been imprisoned on British ships. Among those sent to St. Augustine, Florida, was Josiah Smith Jr., a businessman and Patriot. Smith's father, the Rev. Josiah Smith, had

Right: Martha Milner Phillips, 1856. *Courtesy Natalie Simpson* (B).

Below: Josiah Smith House, 7 Meeting Street. *Courtesy Paul Calhoun.*

Mary Smith, 1795, the wife of Deacon Josiah Smith and daughter-in-law of the Rev. Josiah Smith. *Courtesy Natalie Simpson* (B).

been pastor of the Independent Church from 1734 to 1750. During the occupation of Charleston, Rev. Smith and his son's family refused to take an oath of allegiance to the Crown and were ordered to leave Charleston for Philadelphia in 1781. Meanwhile, after nearly a year of exile in St. Augustine, the younger Smith and others were part of a prisoner exchange and were sent to Philadelphia as well. A total of thirty-eight men from the Independent Church, along with many of their families, were sent into exile.

The bombardment of Charleston began on April 2, 1780. During the interval between the commencement of the shelling and the surrender of the town, the Rev. James Edmonds performed divine service in the church to a few worshippers, mostly women and invalids, for the men were on the lines both night and day. During one service, a cannonball landed in the churchyard.[61] The church was mostly vacant after that until the British left Charleston in 1782. The church, as a consequence of the war, was temporarily disorganized and dispersed. There was no settled minister for six years. The Independent Church, however, functioned in Philadelphia while members were in exile there.

Those years of suffering forged the Independent Church into an instrument that would exert great influence on the political, religious and cultural renaissance of its city after independence. In 1782, acting in astonishing faith, the church-in-exile held a congregational meeting in Philadelphia, where they made arrangements to call a minister, Rev.

Two-year-old Mary Toomer. Dates are missing on the stone, which was damaged by a cannonball during a skirmish in the American Revolution. *Courtesy Missy Loewe* (B).

William Hollinshead, to Charleston "as soon as may be feasible."[62] Rev. Tennent had died in 1777. Members remaining in Charleston began to rebuild the Meeting House during the week of British evacuation. In 1782, "when the British vacated Charleston they left only the shell of the church building. The pulpit and pews were taken down and destroyed, and the empty enclosure used, first as a hospital for the sick, and afterwards as a storehouse for provisions of the royal army." Due to the terrible destruction by the enemy to the interior of the church, it was decided to "repew" and "refloor" the church on Meeting Street.[63]

After the War

A year later, on December 11, 1783, "the day appointed by Congress as a day of thanksgiving to Almighty God for the blessings of peace and independence," the repaired edifice was consecrated anew by its recently arrived pastor, Rev. William Hollinshead.[64] Rev. Isaac S. Keith was called to serve as a co-pastor with the Rev. William Hollinshead at the Independent Meeting House in Charleston in 1788. Rev. Keith was a bachelor when he arrived in Charleston, and married three times while living here. He continued in his role as pastor for twenty-five years, until his death in 1813.

Miles Brewton House, 27 King Street. *Courtesy Paul Calhoun.*

In 1787, as the congregation increased in numbers, work was begun again on the second church building, located on Archdale Street, which had been started during Rev. Tennent's pastorate before the war. The Archdale Street church, which was only half completed at the start of the war, was used to stable the horses of the British army during the occupation. The two churches were served by co-pastors, Revs. Hollinshead and Keith. For thirty years co-pastors preached one sermon in both churches each Sunday, alternating morning and afternoon services.[65]

Many members of the church, both before and after the Revolution, were businessmen of extreme wealth and power. These men and their descendants were instrumental in forming political and economic policy for Charleston, the state and the nation. Josiah Smith Jr. was typical of these men, returning to Charleston with his family from exile and working successfully as a businessman and banker until his death in 1826. He worked equally hard for the church as a deacon for forty years and served as treasurer for over fifty years. In 1789 Smith founded the Clergy Society to establish a fund for the support of disabled ministers and their widows and children. He recognized the need for such a fund as his father, the Rev. Josiah Smith Sr., was disabled for thirty years and had no pension. This society is one of the oldest groups of its kind in the country and has played an important role throughout the history of the church.

After the war members of Circular continued to lead in Charleston, in South Carolina and in the nation. Nathaniel Russell, Richard Hutson (the first mayor of Charleston), the Peronneaus, the DeSaussures, the Bees, the Matthews and the Vanderhorst families were extremely wealthy merchants and planters. H.L. Pinckney and Robert Y. Hayne were important lawyers. Pinckney also owned a plantation on the Cooper River. Henry W. DeSaussure was considered South Carolina's most distinguished legal scholar.[66] Daniel DeSaussure, William Cleland and Hugh Swinton were also prominent members of the church. All of these men built their personal fortunes, but also worked to build their church and city. Some also served at the state and national level of government and finance, and were influential in forming the precepts of the new country.

At the Constitutional Convention in Philadelphia, the South Carolina delegates strongly supported the protection of slavery. John Rutledge of South Carolina said, "Religion and humanity have nothing to do with this question [slavery]. Interest alone is the governing principle of nations." This philosophy was to govern South Carolina and Charleston's views on the subject. The invention of the first water-powered rice mill in 1787 and the cotton gin in 1793 made slavery even more profitable and greatly expanded cultivated land across the Midlands and Upcountry. This meant more slaves, which meant extreme wealth for Charleston's slave traders and merchants.

3.

THIRD CHURCH BUILDING,
1806 TO 1861 AND THEN SOME

During this chapter of church history we see how people dealt with the issues of this stormy period in American history. Amazing hardships were in store for them, but early in the century there were glory days. The church building and congregation reflected the prosperity of the region and the sophisticated cultural aspects of antebellum Charleston. Within fifty-five years, however, the church would be in ruins, both the physical building and its congregation. Momentous political, economic and moral decisions were made here in Charleston, and this period of the church's history gives us a glimpse of the lives of the people who made them, including the members who were slaves dealing with their own ways of facing the world.

This third building would see tremendous changes in its congregation and its surroundings. Charleston was flourishing and so were the church and its members. The time from just after the American Revolution through the 1820s was South Carolina's period of greatest prosperity. This prosperity, however, was rooted in slavery, which would become a bitterly divisive issue and have dire consequences for Charleston and for the church.

By the early 1800s, demand for pews had become so great at the Independent Church that the congregation decided to erect a new church building, on the same site, at a cost of $60,000. While one building was demolished and the other constructed, the congregation worshiped in the South Carolina Society Hall at 72 Meeting Street. The congregation decided to build an entirely new brick edifice. David Ramsay, noted physician, historian and member of Circular, suggested that the new church be in circular form, crediting the idea to his wife, Martha. The building's architect was the nationally celebrated Robert Mills, who designed the Washington monument in Washington, D.C. Circular Church was one of Mills's early designs; he later designed the nation's first fireproof building at 100 Meeting Street—where the South Carolina Historical Society is located

Circular Church and Institute Hall, destroyed by fire in 1861.

Sketch of Circular Church, Institute Hall and Meeting Street, circa 1860. *Courtesy South Carolina Historical Society.*

today—and First Baptist Church at 48 Meeting Street. Construction on this new church was begun in 1804.

The new building was opulent. The round auditorium had a copper dome; there was a portico of six pillars over the sidewalk, a steeple tower sixty feet high, seven doors, twenty-six windows and a gallery encircling the larger part of the auditorium.[67] It had a ten-foot-wide center aisle for serving communion, and accommodated up to two thousand people. The building was lit entirely by candles, and it was said that it took the sexton over two and a half hours to light and extinguish the candles each time the church was illuminated. In May of 1806 the church was opened for public worship. Not many years later, the church acquired the popular title of the "Circular Church."

While none denied the grandeur of the church, there were some mixed reviews. After a visit to Charleston, Yankee preacher Rev. Abiel Abbot wrote in his journal about the new church: "The most extraordinary building on some accounts, I presume to say, in the United States…It was built of Carolina brick with a flagged pavement, the aisles broad…& carpeted to

Circular Church pew rentals record. *Courtesy South Carolina Historical Society.*

prevent echo—the pulpit at the East end, neat & convenient…It is, beyond all comparison, the most difficult to fill with a human voice that I have ever seen & is said to be the coldest house in the winter in this city & the hottest in the summer."[68]

Construction of the new church was begun with inadequate funds and without any subscriptions, but with a strong reliance on Providence that the sale of pews and their yearly rentals, added to the old funds, would raise the required amount. A select 60 pews were sold for $30,390, and the remaining 106 were distributed for a total of $25,550. The church also imposed a yearly rental, which averaged $24 per pew. Thus, more than $50,000 was secured, sufficient with the amount subscribed to defray the entire expense of the building, and an annual income of $3,978 toward defraying the salaries of the ministers and other contingent expenses. In 2007 dollars, members raised over $1 million for the church and the average pew rental was about $500. Seating for the poor may have been a problem, as the Rev. Dr. Isaac S. Keith gave $300 to provide 2 or 3 pews rent-free in the new church to families of the poorer members of the congregation.[69]

Josiah Smith Jr., who was treasurer of the church and president of the Clergy Society at the time, writes in church records:

Current Circular Church pews with hymnals and number tags similar to those used when pews were rented out. *Courtesy Natalie Simpson.*

September 11th, 1806, there was recorded cash received of Joseph Milligan for his purchase of Pew Number (20) in Archdale Church at Publick Outcry [auction] on the 31 August, as the highest Bidder, sold by the church as a forfeited pew, agreeably to the Resolve of Church Meeting on the 3d said Month, being in Arrear for Rent to amount of 17.5 dollars and for which purchase, I this day delegate to Mr. Milligan the Printed deed of conveyance as Established by the Rules of the Church with its Seal of Incorporation thereto affixed, and dated 31 August 1807.

It seems that if you did not pay your pew rental, you lost your pew.

The seal mentioned by Josiah Smith Jr. was commissioned in 1805. Artist Thomas Coram made the silver seal to be used to imprint official church and Clergy Society papers. The seal was rescued from the 1861 fire and can be seen today on display at the Charleston Museum.

In 1816, the Clergy Society established that the allowance for a disabled pastor, a widow or a child should not exceed $1,000 a year.[70] The charter was changed in 1834 to allow the society to give money to Circular Church,[71] something they have done many times in the years since.

Silver Seal, 1805, used to validate official papers. It has a drawing of the new church with the words, "SO CAROLINA CONGREGA CHURCH SOC RELIEF CLERGY INCORP A.D. 1789" marching around the edge. *Courtesy Congregational Church Clergy Society.*

THE TWO CHURCHES SEPARATE

In 1815, a situation arose that would surely test the congregational system of governance of the church. When the young Benjamin Palmer and the older William Hollinshead were the pastors for the two Independent Churches in Charleston, Dr. Hollinshead's health was in decline. He asked for, and got, a nine-month leave of absence. Rev. Anthony Forster, from North Carolina, was engaged as temporary supply. He continued in this capacity after Dr. Hollinshead returned, still disabled. Dr. Hollinshead only lived another year. It was thought that Rev. Forster would be unanimously chosen to co-pastor with Rev. Palmer; however, there arose doubt among some whether Rev. Forster was in accord with the long-accepted doctrines of the church. As a result, on March 3, 1817, a committee was appointed to consider alternate possible candidates.[72]

A special meeting of ninety-five men was called by a group of five men who were all supporters of Rev. Forster. It was proposed by his friends that, in view of the fact that the church was not in harmony about extending a call to Rev. Forster, the rules be revised and that "each of the two churches have a stated pastor," with the majority to take Circular Church and the minority to take Archdale and call Mr. Forster. In addition, it was proposed that there remain one church society.

Before action on this proposal could be taken, however, it was voted to read correspondence between the deacons and Rev. Forster that showed the minister had refused to declare whether he would accept the stated doctrines of the church and called into question their right to ask him. It was moved by Robert Y. Hayne and seconded that "the connection between this Church and the Rev. A. Forster be dissolved and the treasurer be instructed to pay him six months' salary in advance. The motion passed, 58 to 45. Thus the meeting called by his friends to secure the call of Mr. Forster resulted in his ejection from the position of temporary pastor after two years."[73]

The church held a well-advertised meeting attended by 116 men. Several motions were made and rejected. Thomas Lee's suggestion for a committee to study the concept of two independent churches with power to elect their own pastors and to report on the practicability of the plan was accepted, and a committee of 5 from each side of the controversy was formed.

The committee formed what was called a "convention" to carry out the division. Two groups worked independently to develop what each considered to be the terms of the division. Remarkably, both groups proposed exactly the same terms "as the most likely to tranquillize the Church and unite in brotherly love all its Worshippers."[74]

The recommendation was accepted unanimously. The report was read from the pulpit the next Sunday, and the two papers were signed, there being eighty-nine names to remain in Circular Church and sixty-two to belong to Archdale Street Church. Each church would function independently. Those who joined what became the Second Independent Congregational Church of Charleston were "influenced more directly by eighteenth-century rationalism."[75] The death of Rev. Forster occurred about one year after the separation. That church then called Dr. Samuel Gilman, a Unitarian minister from Boston. However, the Second Independent Church did not begin using the name Unitarian until the 1830s. The ongoing Dissenter spirit of the church was evident in its support of those who wished to form a new church. Also evident was the lack of any external control, either Congregational or Presbyterian.

In 1821 a building was erected in the yard for use by the first Sunday school in South Carolina, started by Dr. Benjamin Palmer, who was pastor at that time. At first it was managed independent of the church. It was a union school, including Baptists, Congregationalists and Presbyterians. When it was reorganized in 1834, a vote of the church placed the Sunday school under the care and supervision of the Circular Congregational Church. There was to be a male superintendent elected annually by a majority of the teachers present; there were also to be a male assistant superintendent elected by the male teachers and a female assistant superintendent elected by the female teachers.[76] This was probably the first recognition of women as having any official position connected with the church.

Unitarian Church at 4 Archdale Street. *Courtesy Paul Calhoun.*

After more than thirty years with no significant steeple, the church decided, in 1838, to add one "on the present tower, at a cost of $6,000.00," perhaps to put a stop to the rhyme that was circulating among the wits of the time:

> *Charleston is a pious place and full of pious people;*
> *They built a house on Meeting Street*
> *But could not raise the steeple.*

The new steeple was 120 feet tall, and was built on the base tower of 60 feet, raising the total to 180 feet from the ground! It was painted yellow, in contrast to the red at the bottom. This color combination did not sit well with a number of Charleston's citizens. The criticism of the original color of the church, red, was harsh even before the yellow was added. At that time it was felt that white, green or stone were the only acceptable colors for a church.

Many people thought that Mills's church was a failed building architecturally. Rev. Abbot's 1806 words about the coldness of the new church building proved to be correct. He was also right about the acoustics, which were acceptable for music, but terrible for speaking. It was felt that

Sketch of the Circular Church designed in 1804 by Robert Mills, done by the architect of the renovations, Edward C. Jones, in 1853. *Courtesy South Carolina Historical Society.*

some elements of the design did not mesh with others, particularly the style of the columns. So in 1853, only forty-one years after the building's completion, a thorough renovation of the church was done with $18,000 appropriated from the Clergy Society. The society also paid $6,500 beyond the original estimate, "to insure the church's safety and durability and to render it an architectural ornament to the city."[77] The church building, "with its pillared entrance, lofty spire, elaborate lighting system, pipe organ and marble memorials on the inner walls, was considered one of the finest buildings in the South."[78]

From 1853 until 1858 plans were drawn up and funds were raised for renovation of the lecture hall on the rear of the property. In 1859 the renovations and second-story addition to the lecture hall were completed. This building also served as the site for the Sunday school.

ISSUES OF SLAVERY

Southern whites defended slavery as sanctioned by the Bible and natural law, and Southern religious leaders were among the leading defenders. Churches in the Lowcountry preached that the Bible sanctioned slavery and that slaves should be obedient to their masters. They also taught that masters should treat their slaves well. Reformed churches such as Circular found themselves increasingly at odds with their brethren in the North and in Great Britain. Many Quakers, who were early opponents of slavery, left the South before the war because of ongoing hostility toward them.[79]

In these early antebellum years leading up to the Civil War, as white Congregationalists and Presbyterians struggled with their strong sense of duty and their concern for "right" thinking, they began to turn with increasing vigor to the task of seeing that slaves received "proper" religious instruction, especially as the attacks against slavery grew in intensity. Classes in religious education were established at Circular by Rev. Dr. Benjamin Palmer, who was minister from 1814 until 1835, for blacks who wished to become members of Circular Church. Records indicate there were between 200 and 330 "Seekers," as prospective black members who attended classes were called, from 1822 to 1835.[80] After all-black churches were banned in Charleston in 1834, several hundred blacks chose to worship at Circular.

The legal system tried to maintain strict control of the black community. After the Vesey rebellion, black churches were forbidden and black religious leaders in white churches, sometimes called "exhorters," could not go under the designation of "preacher," but they could lead their classes with prayer and singing. Much responsibility was given to these black leaders, especially at Circular, where records show that white members were not always there to oversee the groups even though the law stipulated that they must be present. These leaders were powerful men in the black community, and many were free men.

One of the responsibilities of the black leaders was to visit, as a pastor might, in the homes of the black membership. If a member was found to be destitute, leaders could recommend that help be provided out of the congregation's "poor funds." When deacons or other officers of the congregation approved such recommendations, the black leaders were given authority to deliver a small stipend and other aid to the one in need. At Circular an average of $375 yearly was distributed to the needy members of the congregation throughout the antebellum period, approximately half to black and half to white members.[81]

At that time the church played a disciplinary role for all of its members, black and white. People could be expelled for certain behaviors like adultery, or be reprimanded for lesser crimes such as drunkenness. The board of the church had the final decision, but frequently relied on the black leaders to make the judgment when the defendant was black.

In a time when slaves had to come to terms with their roles in life, it must have been a blessing to have a church and these black leaders to turn to. Many times, however, decisions in their lives were complicated by the fact that slavery defied moral logic and there was no clear resolution to a problem. For example, Mary Holway, a slave member of Circular, wanted to remarry, but asked the church board for permission as her first husband had been sold away from her six years previously. The board seemed unable to resolve this moral dilemma set up by slavery, for their decision was to leave it up to Mary.[82]

It seems reasonable to assume that Rev. Palmer was helping slaves learn to read. He kept a diary or "personal minute book" of the spiritual education classes that he held for black members. Since teaching slaves to read was illegal, he does not specify that it was part of the curriculum, but he kept notes on all of the "Seekers." He noted which ones could read and which ones were learning to read. He also gave the classes pamphlets for spiritual education that advocated learning to read. These pamphlets were meant to be read to the slaves, but Palmer gave them to the leaders to work with and thus was giving them material with which they could teach reading. The act of joining a church was one of the few important personal, social decisions slaves could make for themselves. Those African Americans who chose to join Circular were probably drawn by its open and flexible view of faith, its school led by Rev. Palmer and its spirit of welcoming a variety of beliefs.[83]

The census of 1820 showed more black than white persons in South Carolina, which would make it the only state with a clear black majority for the next one hundred years. In the Lowcountry, blacks outnumbered whites by several times. This, perhaps, accounted for the hysteria over the supposed Denmark Vesey plot in 1822. Vesey was a slave who had bought his freedom and worked as a carpenter. He planned a revolt that was to lead to a mass exodus of black families to Haiti. Supposedly, they were to kill their masters and fight their way to the docks in Charleston Harbor. A slave in Charleston warned his master, and Vesey was found out. A total of 131 people were arrested; 35, including Vesey, were found guilty and hanged; and 37 were exiled to Cuba. Vesey was an early member of and lay preacher with the Emanuel AME Church in Charleston, which had over 3,000 members. The church's pastor was Morris Brown. After the uprising, the building was razed by the city. Vesey's son, Robert, rebuilt it in 1865.[84]

One of Vesey's lieutenants was a member of Circular Church. His name is unknown. This person had the coveted position of going around and lighting all of the candles every Sunday. He was a respected member of the church and was identified as a leader of the rebellion. Many members were slaveholders and were devastated and terrified during this time. In letters from Mary Lamboll Thomas Beach, a member of Circular and daughter of the Rev. John Thomas, to her sister Elizabeth Lamboll Gilchrist, Mary

Fence at the Miles Brewton House. It is said that spike-topped fences were added to houses in Charleston to protect against rebellious slaves following the Denmark Vesey insurrection. *Courtesy Paul Calhoun.*

discusses the events surrounding the time of the trial and executions of the slaves involved in the planned Vesey slave rebellion. In them she writes about how all the townsmen were asked to serve on patrols, even Dr. Palmer, Circular's pastor. She speculates that pastors should be exempt, and in a July 23, 1822 letter she writes that Dr. Palmer had sent a substitute. She also writes, "I hope it is a time of much prayer here—the Tuesday afternoon meeting is very full generally, and almost to crowding at times and there the prayers are under less restraint on account of no blacks being present." She also discusses how several church members' slaves were among those to be executed. Of her own slaves she writes,

> *Ours as yet have not been implicated as I have heard in the slightest manner, but this is no security that some of them may not finish on the gallows in ten days. But oh! This business I fear is akin to the French Revolution to think that many of these people growing up like children, as is the case of many of the condemned, could be brought to such a fiend like temper that they would commit to embrace their hands in the blood of their masters and their little sons who never could have shed theirs.*

She goes on to say, prophetically, "Ah! Slavery is a hard business and I am afraid we shall in this country have it to our bitter cost some day or other."[85]

As slavery and states' rights arguments swirled, and people like Mary Lamboll Thomas Beach grew increasingly uneasy, life went on. Circular Church members contributed to life in Charleston and their church in a variety of ways.

MINISTRY

During the nineteenth century, the impact of women on the church seems to have been for their philanthropy and good works rather than for any official role, as they were still not voting members. In 1816, women of the congregation formed the Congregational and Presbyterian Female Association for Assisting in the Education of Pious Young Men for the Gospel Ministry; the name was later changed to the Ladies Home Missionary Society. The primary end of the organization was education. Its secondary purpose was Christian work. The Missionary Society is thought to be the oldest state charter of South Carolina and was active until the later part of the twentieth century.

In 1836, Rev. Reuben Post came to Circular. A Vermonter, he prepared for the ministry at Princeton. He brought a great deal of political knowledge with him, as he had previously been elected chaplain of the United States Senate. He was very active in united meetings held by the evangelical churches in Charleston, and his pastorate was filled with building projects. His ministry to the congregation, however, was the reason he was most beloved. In 1857, Dr. Post took a long vacation in the North, at the urging of the congregation. While he was gone a serious epidemic broke out in the city. Although sickness and death were widespread, Dr. Post returned home, long before he was expected, too worried about his congregation to remain away any longer. In a short time he also fell victim to the pestilence and died in the twenty-third year of his pastorate. The church was draped in black for six months after his death, and a marble tablet to his memory was placed on the inside wall. His gravestone is in the churchyard, along with those of his wife and daughter. They are in the shape of chess pieces: the king, queen and rook.

MEMBERS OF NOTE

During this time, Circular's members continued to be influential not only in Charleston, but also in the state and nation. Membership included

Portrait of Rev. Reuben Post by Thomas Sully. *Courtesy South Carolina Historical Society.*

politicians, writers, publishers, planters, builders and extremely wealthy merchants. They were the "movers and shakers" of Charleston during these years. Sketches of a cross section of these people serve to give us a taste of the congregation and their contributions to Circular, to Charleston and to the country.

Early in the period of the third church building, in 1815, the church lost one of its most prominent and beloved members, David Ramsay, a physician and historian. He had been appointed by the courts to pass on the mental condition of one William Linner, a deranged tailor who was making threats against the judges, lawyers and jurors who ruled against him in court. Ramsay found him to be insane, and recommended he be kept confined. He was released instead, and he shot Ramsay on the street near St. Michael's Church. As he lay dying, Ramsay declared to friends that Linner was insane and could not be held responsible for the attack. This, and the fact that he left a 236-page book of records of unpaid medical bills owed him over the preceding seven years, testify to his generosity. His children, however, were left nearly destitute. His daughter, Catherine, and two other unmarried daughters opened a school for girls at the Ramsay family home at 92 Broad Street in order to support themselves and their brothers. In 1816, their situation was mitigated when they received $23,000 for land that their mother had inherited from Henry Laurens.

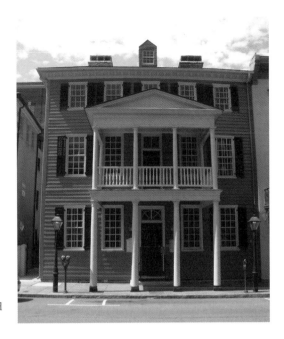

David Ramsey House at 92 Broad Street. *Courtesy Paul Calhoun.*

Robert Y. Hayne was a well-known and politically influential member of Circular Church. Born in Charleston in 1791, Hayne was unable to go to college because of family financial problems. He studied law with Langdon Cheves and was admitted to the bar before he was twenty-one. His financial fortune improved with marriages into two wealthy Charleston families. He married Frances Pinckney in 1813 and, after her death, Rebecca Brewton Alston in 1820. Hayne was Speaker of the South Carolina House of Representatives in 1814. He was also state attorney general and was elected to the U.S. Senate. He became a states' rights advocate in the late 1820s. For two weeks in 1830, he and Daniel Webster had a series of debates. Hayne defended the radical states' rights doctrine of nullification, slavery and the sale of Western land. In 1832, "Hayne turned his Senate seat over to John C. Calhoun, nullification's architect, and was rewarded with the governor's chair of South Carolina."[86] Hayne also served as mayor of Charleston from 1835 to 1837.

Richard Yeadon helped shape the thinking and educational development of Charleston through his writing and his leadership. He was a lawyer and part owner and editor of the *Charleston Daily Courier*. Even though he was a leading Unionist before the war, he gave generously to equip Southern soldiers and build a navy. He served three terms in the South Carolina House of Representatives, originated an ordinance that established the Charleston High School and strongly supported the College of Charleston. He died in 1870.

Richard Yeadon, 1870, the writer and activist who is buried next to his wife Mary, 1871. The two graves were recently moved to the front of the church. *Courtesy Paul Calhoun* (A1).

Daniel Stevens was the great-grandson of New England preacher Cotton Mather. Stevens lost two wives and five children by the time he was thirty. He was imprisoned by the British in 1781, was in irons for two months in the Exchange Building and was then taken to a prison ship before being exchanged. He ultimately achieved the rank of colonel. He was elected high sheriff for Charleston District for three years, senator for St. Luke's Parish for six years and Charleston intendant (mayor) in 1819–20.[87]

Deacon Andrew P. Gready was a quiet hero of the church as he preserved much of its history and ministered to its poor by supervising church benevolences. He served the church as deacon for over thirty years, as treasurer for twenty and was supervising sexton for many years. In 1990, a document by Mr. Gready was found in which he recorded all burials from 1844 to 1897. He included "remarks" including the burial plot (e.g. Peronneau), how the person died (lockjaw) or the person's job (carpenter, clerk, deacon). The document is housed at the South Carolina Historical Society.

The Bennett family is a good example of social action continuing through generations as the family fortune is amassed. Thomas Bennett (1754–1814), the father of Governor Thomas Bennett Jr. (1781–1863), was a contractor and designer of public buildings. He owned a lumberyard and a rice mill and was a prominent member of Circular Church for forty years. He built the first circular-shaped church in 1804–06. His company designed and built the Charleston Orphan House between 1792 and 1794 to meet the needs of the many orphan children in the city due to yellow fever epidemics.

Governor Thomas Bennett Jr. and his wife Mary, also members of the church, had another connection to the orphan house. They had a son named Washington Jefferson, but after three of their other young children died between 1807 and 1812, the Bennetts decided to adopt nine-year-old Christopher Memminger, who had been orphaned when his German immigrant parents died of yellow fever. As adults, Washington Jefferson Bennett and Memminger maintained an interest in education. Bennett continued in his father's lumberyard business and is said to have planned the Free School on St. Philip Street in 1855, later to become Bennett School. Memminger, perhaps most widely known for his service as secretary of the treasury for the Confederacy, was a lawyer and became a member of the South Carolina State Legislature. In 1854 he reorganized the state's educational system, and he was also one of the founders of the public school system in Charleston. Memminger Elementary School and auditorium are named after him.

Washington Jefferson Bennett, like his father Thomas, adopted an orphan boy, seventeen-year-old Andrew Buist Murray (1844–1928), who had grown up in the Charleston Orphan House. Murray later married his adopted sister, Mary Bennett, and became a partner with his two adopted Bennett brothers in the family's rice and lumber companies. As a highly successful businessman who made a large fortune, he was a generous philanthropist. In addition to many charities, he developed Murray Boulevard. The area behind the waterfront boulevard at that time embraced forty-seven acres of mud flats between the original shoreline and the sea wall, from the west end of White Point Gardens to the west end of Tradd Street. The city filled in the mud flats in this area and the tract was developed into building lots. At Murray's suggestion, East Battery was linked with the new boulevard by extending the sea wall south of White Point Gardens, creating a riverside drive over a mile long, named Murray Boulevard, after him. Murray contributed about 50 percent of the cost of the development.[88] This is now some of the priciest real estate in Charleston.

Mary Bennett, 1832, wife of Thomas Bennett Jr., governor of South Carolina. *Courtesy Natalie Simpson* (A1).

CHANGES IN CHURCH FORTUNE: WAR, FIRE AND EARTHQUAKE

Even before the Civil War, Charleston and Circular were faced with severe challenges to their survival. One of these, a resentment of the church's connection to the Northern Congregationalists, was beginning to surface in 1859, when the Rev. Thomas O. Rice, a Congregational minister from Brighton, Massachusetts, was chosen pastor. This was about a month and a half after John Brown's raid on Harpers Ferry, West Virginia, and Northerners were looked upon with suspicion in much of the South. From its beginning, Circular had a history of Northern ministers and a record of supporting ministerial students in Northern colleges. In these years before

Circular Church, Institute Hall and the Teetotal Restaurant, circa 1860.

Circular Church ruins after the 1861 fire. *Both photographs courtesy South Carolina Historical Society.*

Circular Church ruins with front column on Meeting Street. *Courtesy Library of Congress.*

and after the Civil War, association with Northerners was not desirable; gradually, these allegiances would play a part in the church's ability to recruit and retain members.[89]

While the war had not yet begun, preparations for it were affecting the church. At the January 1861 Annual Meeting, the following statement was made: "In consequence of the present political and commercial state of affairs, we have not pressed subscriptions in the congregation, knowing that the pecuniary means of most are curtailed and that much has been given in the city to aid in preparation to defend the State."[90]

The actual war began on April 12, 1861, with the firing on Fort Sumter. Just nine months later, on December 11, 1861, as the congregation was trying to cope with the war, an even more severe blow to Circular Church came in the form of a great fire, which deprived the congregation of its church sanctuary building for thirty years. It swept away all buildings in its path, destroying not only Circular and its lecture hall, but several other churches as well. The fire also destroyed Institute Hall, next to Circular Church, the scene of the 1860 Democratic National Convention and the place where the Ordinance of Secession was signed.

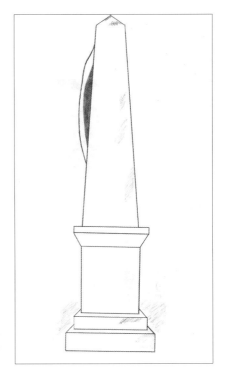

Sketch of the bent slab tomb, showing the side of the slab bent by the intense heat of the fire, sketched from a drawing that appeared in a story about Circular's history in the *Sunday News*, Charleston, February 19, 1888. *Courtesy Lisa Hayes.*

Emma Holmes, a twenty-three-year-old descendant of early church members, described the fire at length in her diary:

> *The flames swept on with inconceivable rapidity & fierceness, notwithstanding the almost superhuman efforts of the firemen…Throughout that awful night, we watched the weary hours at the windows and still the flames leaped madly on with demoniac fury…At five a.m. the city was wrapped in a living wall of fire from the Cooper to the Ashley without a single gap to break its dread uniformity. It seemed as if the day would never dawn…when the sun rose, the fire was still raging so fiercely that its glare almost overpowered that of the sun…The wind circled in eddies, driving the flames in every direction & carrying showers of flakes to an immense distance…The Circular Church is where all my ancestors worshipped and are buried for 175 years [sic]…A few years ago [it was] thoroughly done up & refurnished, making it the largest and one of the handsomest churches in the city.* [91]

Some of the gravestones near the church were cracked by the intense heat when the church burned. One tomb even had one side bowed from

81

Newer, shorter shaft of the bent slab tomb of Mrs. Eliza Catherine Bryan, 1842. *Courtesy Natalie Simpson* (A1).

the heat.[92] This marble slab from the tomb nearest the church, which was "warped by the intense heat of the burning building until it was bent like a bow," formed the north side of the monument's shaft erected to the memory of Mrs. Catherine Bryan, daughter of Solomon Legare, who was the mother of nine sons and twelve daughters.[93]

"The iron, copper, and bell metal of the ruined building were salvaged, but the brick walls and tower were destined to remain standing for many years."[94] All that was saved from the fire were the baptismal font—which is still in use by the church today—a collection of antique silver church serving pieces, a seal, a hymnal and a Bible, printed by John Baskerville, Cambridge University printer from 1758 to 1768. The Baskerville Bible is considered one of the finest books printed during the eighteenth century. (Circular's copy is on loan to the Charleston Museum.)

In her diary, Emma Holmes writes of a feeling in Charleston after the fire that "the shock has been so great in extent, so sudden and so awful, that private feelings seemed merged into public feeling, and each one seems to forget their own losses to regret that of their friends."[95] This was apparently true of church congregations, also. Offers for use of their buildings came from the Glebe Street Presbyterian Church, Central Presbyterian Church, the First Presbyterian Church and the Unitarian Church. The Second Presbyterian Church, in offering their sympathy and the use of their building, recalled that many of their members had been fellow members or

Baptismal font given by Mrs. Jane Keith, the widow of Rev. Isaac Keith, in 1847. *Courtesy Natalie Simpson.*

descendants of those who founded the Circular Church.[96] Following the fire the congregation met in Hibernian Hall, the lecture room of the Central Presbyterian Church and in the Orphan House Chapel.

Church members, many of whom had lost everything, put aside personal loss and quickly gathered at Hibernian Hall on the Sunday following the fire. Resolutions adopted at that meeting expressed their unabated affection and appreciation of the old organization handed down to them from their fathers, who had planted this church in the wilderness and pledged themselves to restore their house of worship.[97]

Circumstances were becoming more and more difficult for the church. In 1864, Rev. Thomas O. Rice resigned and sought passage through Confederate and Union lines to return home to Boston, leaving the congregation without a minister.[98] After the fire the church asked that the income from investments of the Clergy Society be given to the church, and this was done.[99] Investments of the society were largely in bonds. Luckily, the society had invested only a small portion of its funds in Confederate bonds during the Civil War. Times were still very difficult financially for church members due to the failure of members' businesses because of the war and the fire.

Federal troops did not occupy Charleston until near the end of the war. The blockade, however, made it difficult to transact trade, and businesses were hit hard. There were battles nearby and families lost husbands and

David Ramsay, 1863, grandson of Dr. David Ramsay. *Courtesy Natalie Simpson* (C).

children; poverty was rampant. When Union soldiers occupied Charleston in 1865, many of the finer houses were confiscated and life was difficult for all Charlestonians. Many citizens lined up daily for rations issued by Union soldiers to keep from starving. Dr. David Ramsay's grandson was one of the members of Circular who died in the Civil War.

While the defeat of the Confederacy was a tragedy to white members of Circular, it meant freedom for the majority of the population of the Lowcountry. Slaves were now free. Blacks celebrated for weeks in Charleston. Congregational missionaries immediately flocked to South Carolina to minister to the freedmen. Henry Ward Beecher, a Northern Congregationalist minister who was a staunch abolitionist, preached in Charleston on April 13, 1865, just days after the war ended.[100] Led by these Northern Congregationalists, blacks at Circular were urged to form their own church, which they did in 1867; 117 African American members left to go to Plymouth, whose very name evoked New England Congregationalism.[101] The American Missionary Society of New York established Avery Normal Institute, the first fully accredited secondary school for African Americans in Charleston. Northern missionaries also founded schools like Penn Center in Beaufort.

Plymouth Congregational Church, 124 Spring Street, founded in 1865. This is a newer building, not the original church. *Courtesy Paul Calhoun.*

Since Circular Church had always been independent of any national organization and was firmly Southern in outlook, these Northern Congregationalists must have been deeply resented by many members. By prior association, though, the Circular congregation must also have been connected in the minds of Charlestonians with the Northern Congregationalists who were anathema to whites in the South after the war. This made it very difficult to recruit and retain members. "Circular Congregational Church moved from a central place in Charleston's economic, political and cultural life to the edges."[102]

Rebuilding Years

The fire, the Civil War and the loss of members due to emancipation and Circular's affiliation with the Northern Congregationalists made rebuilding Circular a difficult task. It would take a determined core of members thirty years, with many setbacks, to do so. In 1866, thirteen members met and voted to rebuild the lecture room using securities still held by the church to cover the cost.[103] The building was ready for use in 1867.[104] Members

Ruins of Circular Church after 1865, with scaffolding to keep bricks from falling. *Courtesy Library of Congress.*

worshipped there for eighteen years until, in 1885, a cyclone (hurricane) tore the roof off the new two-story chapel, or lecture hall. On August 31, 1886, an earthquake brought destruction to both the church and the city. The lecture hall was so shaken as to be unusable and major repairs had to be made. The earthquake also made the ruins of the sanctuary building unsafe, so that the remaining bricks had to be taken down and saved. This cleared the way for the eventual building of the new church.

When the bricks of the ruined church were finally taken down, bats, birds and landscape artists mourned. The bats had made a substantial colony in the ruins, many birds nested and many artists loved to paint the romantic scene of the ruined church amid the graveyard. In the January 19, 1888 edition of the *Charleston Sunday News*, an article about "The Old Circular Church" reports, in the sentimental writing style of the times, that for years the ruins had been

> *one of the most interesting and treasured landmarks of a city noted for its relics of "the olden time" until the picturesque pile has almost supplanted the once imposing structure in the memory of the public. Men have come and men have gone, but these venerable ruins have stood on as if loath to sever another link in the chain of memories that still binds us to the irrevocable past.*

Rear of Circular Church in the 1860s. *Courtesy Library of Congress.*

Between the war years and the earthquake, the next crisis came when the church was still in ruins and trying to come to terms with its reduced circumstances. A new pastor, Rev. William H. Adams, was hired in 1867 to lead in rebuilding the church and the congregation. He was a surprising choice, as he was from New England.

Rev. Adams's pastorate was filled with strife and division. The conflict between the pastor and the corporation of the church, which began in 1876, was said to be "the most disastrous event that occurred in the church's history." Rev. George N. Edwards described the impact of the controversy by saying that "nothing had so marred the church's spirit, depleted its membership, and hindered its growth as this controversy." He ranked it above the suffering from the fire of 1861, from pestilence and from a serious division of its membership by the Unitarian separation.[105]

The trouble broke out in April 1876 over the administration of the Sunday school. Rev. Adams suggested the introduction of the new International Uniform Lessons; this was not approved. It was contended with some heat that the pastor had no authority to supervise the Sunday school. Rev. Adams then laid the matter before a Sunday morning congregation to get their opinions on the matter. This was viewed by the governing board of the church as an attempt to subvert their decision. It should be reiterated here that in the Congregationalist tradition, each church practices congregational governance, in which each congregation independently and autonomously runs its own affairs. When the Rev. Adams tried to skirt the decision of the administration of the Sunday school, he was going contrary to Congregational and Circular Church tradition. It is also likely that his Northern background was held against him by the board.

The next major challenge of Rev. Adams's pastorate related to the need for a new building to replace the ruins of the old Circular Church, a grand though sad memorial of the past, which seemed to pose an obstacle to a number of schemes the building committee devised for a new structure on its site. Plans were submitted and adopted, motions were passed and then rejected. Finally the building committee was discharged. It should be remembered that these years were a period of great financial depression throughout the country. For now, the building fund was put in the hands of the church treasurer, to be held in reserve, and the plans were turned over to the president of the church for safekeeping. When Rev. Adams's father, a minister in Boston, sent hymnals for the church to use, Rev. Adams's opponents refused them, and the hymnals were put aside.

A few months later, at the semiannual meeting in July, the church council reported that the pastor had defied the constitution and bylaws of the church by calling for a mixed meeting of the church, in which female members were included, to consider a matter already settled by the male communing members. The council voted to demand the resignation of Rev. Adams, who was visiting his father in New England at the time. He answered their letter with his own, refusing to resign.

During the pastor's absence, new locks and keys were installed by the council to secure the building and it was voted that the pastor's salary cease on August 31, 1876. Rev. Adams returned and demanded that the church doors be opened on December 10. This demand was refused, but legal proceedings, petitions, requests and further demands were rampant.

Next, the council voted that (1) the church be opened for "regular" services and Sabbath school, (2) they reduce the minister's salary from $1,800 to $100 per year and (3) they rent no more pews until the desired harmony be restored. A motion was made that tried to suspend communion service because there was too much contention among the members and those who gathered around the Lord's table, but it lost by the deciding vote of the moderator, Rev. Adams. The congregation was divided, with a bare majority being against the pastor. From this point on, the opponents of Rev. Adams absented themselves from communion and most other services. Because proper procedures were not followed, the pastor hung on for two years. His salary had been cut to almost nothing by those in control, yet members of the congregation continued to support him with individual gifts.

THE REV. WILLIAM H. ADAMS.

Portrait of Rev. William Adams. *Courtesy South Carolina Historical Society.*

Another attempt at ending the dispute was made by securing advice from three ministers of the city who traced the entire trouble back to the unofficial meeting called by the pastor. The end of the long struggle came in April 1878, when Rev. Adams presented his resignation to the corporation, in which he expressed concern for the church's survival. The inevitable consequence of the resignation of the pastor was the loss of many members of the church, though not at once.[106]

The church did survive, however, and in 1879 Rev. A.H. Missildine became pastor. During his tenure the church showed growth, but had financial difficulties that led to his leaving, as he could not support his family on his salary. He wrote a short pamphlet history of the church, a copy of which is buried in a cornerstone of the current sanctuary building.

In 1888, Rev. Henry M. Grant became pastor. His chief task would be the gathering of funds for a new church. On April 13, 1888, the *Charleston News and Courier* printed an article reporting a suggestion that after the debris was removed a park should be built on the site. The church refused. In 1890, Rev. Grant wrote an appeal contained in a pamphlet, *Circular Church*, delineating the church's history. He begins by reminding readers

Appeal for funds that appeared in a fundraising pamphlet by Rev. Henry M. Grant. *Courtesy South Carolina Historical Society.*

that the church is "widely known and honored as having been, for nearly two centuries, the outpost of Congregationalism in the Southern States." The history tells of more than twenty ministers of the gospel who were "reared within its fold," and the "marked moral and religious enterprises of the church, including the first Sunday-school in South Carolina, and the Charleston Bible Society which preceded the American Bible Society by six years." He also remarks that, in addition to other charities previously mentioned in this book, the "Charleston Port Society, older by several years than the American Seamen's Friends' Society, had its birth, and for many years held its anniversaries, in the Old Circular Church" among others. Grant closes by explaining the need for funds due to the fact that "among other vicissitudes, beneficent funds of this church, once signal and varied, have suffered great shrinkage, or total loss, through repeated depreciation or failure of Southern securities consequent upon the Civil War." This time the appeal for funds was successful enough to result in the new Circular Church, which is in use today.

4.

FOURTH CHURCH BUILDING, 1892 TO THE PRESENT

"May this church long stand, not only as a monument to filial zeal, but as a witness that the truth for which the fathers exiled themselves across unknown seas, to savage wilds, has lost none of its preciousness to their children."
–Speech by Rev. Dr. C.S. Vedder of the Huguenot Church at the dedication of the new Circular Church, as reported in the Charleston News & Courier, *January 18, 1892*

At the dawn of the twentieth century, Circular Church was in a very different position than in the past. Gone were the days of opulence and prosperity and the days of having the largest congregation in Charleston. Returning to the spirit of its early roots, it would struggle to stay alive and to find its new identity. It would change from a Dissenter church that had become one of the most powerful churches in the South to a small Dissenter church once again. The congregation's choice of building style seemed to reflect the new role of the church: smaller and less grand, but with flair and integrity. Its sturdiness and the new H.H. Richardson–influenced architecture, chosen over a more traditional Southern style, seemed to proclaim that whatever the congregation had lost, it was ready to meet the challenges of the new century.

On August 5, 1890, nearly thirty years after the previous church burned, a contract was made for building a new church. Cornerstone laying ceremonies were held on Thanksgiving Day 1890. A copper box wrapped in asbestos was placed in the south curve of the wall at the juncture of the southwest vestibule with the main wall. It contains a church history by Rev. A.H. Missildine (1882), a historical sketch by Rev. H.M. Grant (1890), lists of various officers and members, articles of faith, an old memorandum of the laying of the cornerstone in 1804, copies of current newspapers, a directory of Charleston and various coins. This copper box was laid in place by Master Keith Brown, a child of the sixth generation from Deacon Josiah

Left: Circular Church and Bike Shop in the snow, circa 1900.

Below: View of Circular Church with Meeting Street streetcar tracks, 1910. *Both photographs courtesy South Carolina Historical Society.*

View of Circular Church, 1930s.

View of Circular Church, 1950s. *Both photographs courtesy Library of Congress.*

Modern view of rear of Circular Church.

Circular Church with St. Philip's in the background. Both churches were founded in 1681. *Both photographs courtesy Ron Rocz.*

Aerial view of Circular Church looking toward King Street. *Courtesy Ron Rocz.*

"Circular Birdegational Church," one of the oldest oaks in downtown Charleston. *Courtesy Natalie Simpson* (D).

Above: View of side yard with Lance Hall, built in 1859, in background. *Courtesy Ron Rocz* (A1).

Right: Circular section of the "Gateway Walk." *Courtesy Natalie Simpson.*

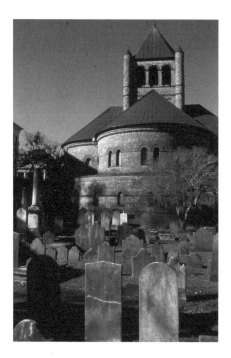

Left: Rear view of Circular Church. *Right* Wrought-iron design and shadow on Lance Hall stair landing. *Both photographs courtesy Natalie Simpson.*

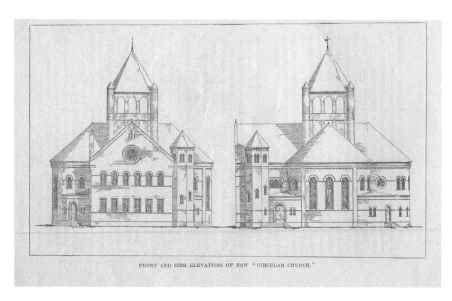

FRONT AND SIDE ELEVATIONS OF NEW "CIRCULAR CHURCH."

Proposed plan of front and side elevations of new Circular Church building. *Courtesy South Carolina Historical Society.*

Wrought-iron stairs leading to Lance Hall.

Front view of Circular Church. *Both photographs courtesy Natalie Simpson*.

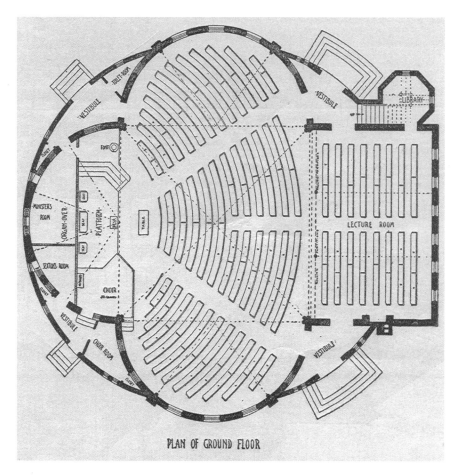

PLAN OF GROUND FLOOR

Proposed plan of ground floor for the new Circular building. Note the differences in use of space in the peripheral areas. *Courtesy South Carolina Historical Society*.

Smith, who laid the cornerstone of the old Circular Church on July 14, 1804.[107] The 1890 box is still buried within the current church walls.

Excerpts from the building's description by its architects, Stephenson & Greene of New York City, describe the building as having a

> *low, circular wall, which in this design encloses the Greek cross and affords space for the several vestibules, and makes the outline of the building almost a circle, conforms to the general style of the rest of the building, and retains the appropriateness of the time-honored name of the church. The main auditorium has a lofty, curved ceiling, and is amply lighted by six large windows and eight small ones. A staircase in the octagonal tower leads*

from the vestibule to the gallery and class-rooms over the lecture-room. The building is to be built of old brick from the old "Circular Church." These brick are unusually large, and are a deep rich brown in color. The large central lantern is to be of wood covered with stained cut shingles. All the wood-work of the interior is designed to be of Georgia and North Carolina pine, and to be stained a dull, rich color.[108]

The twentieth century at Circular was a period of continuing the struggle to maintain a congregation and a church building—no small feat, given the fact that the congregation was impoverished due to the economic ruin brought about by the Civil War, its aftermath and the Great Depression of 1929. This century was also a time when the church would be asked to face the extreme social issues of American society. Circular found its new identity as it faced these challenges.

MAINTAINING THE CHURCH

Circular struggled to stay alive during the first fifty years of the twentieth century. Church records of 1912 show that there were only twenty-eight male (voting) members and sixty-one female (non-voting) members. In 1917, twenty-five years after the new building was completed, the congregation was still struggling to stay afloat financially. During the pastorate of Rev. George Evans Paddack, the church voted to temporarily affiliate with the Congregational Home Ministry Society in New York so that the society could supplement the salary of the pastor. The purpose of this society was to supplement churches in the United States and its territories until they could become financially self-sufficient. Circular Church had fallen financially into the status of a mission church even before the Great Depression. In 1926, Rev. George Edwards came to Circular when Rev. Paddack resigned. His salary, too, was supplemented by the Congregational Home Ministry Society. The organization also provided a special assistant during Rev. Edwards's first two years to help in his work. After Rev. Edwards was disabled by an attack of cerebral thrombosis in 1940, he received a pension from the Circular Church Clergy Society, and for the next six years, he combed through all of the old records of the church and wrote *A History of the Independent or Congregational Church of Charleston, South Carolina, Commonly Known as Circular Church.*

During the Depression, the church was barely holding on. The congregation sacrificed for its love of music in 1930 when it sold $2,000 worth of antique silver to raise money for a pipe organ. The silver included

Above: Sanctuary and pews of current Circular Church.

Below: Ceiling and windows above sanctuary. *Both photographs courtesy Natalie Simpson.*

Pews of Circular Church. *Courtesy Ron Rocz.*

Rose medallion window. *Courtesy Natalie Simpson.*

Stained-glass window. *Courtesy Natalie Simpson.*

Pews. *Courtesy Ron Rocz.*

Right: Open door to the churchyard. *Courtesy Ron Rocz.*

Below: Rev. George Nelson Edwards, 1953. *Courtesy Natalie Simpson* (A1).

a tankard made in 1760, donated by Josiah and Mary Smith.[109] The organ console was adroitly fitted into the space originally intended for the choir, and the major part of the organ was placed in the upper gallery, in front of the six small windows of the sanctuary.[110] In 1933, the mortgage given to this church in 1891 to complete the new building was renewed to 1991, which provides more evidence of the church's poverty. As most mortgages are paid off by the end of the term, the fact that Circular's wasn't indicates that the church had not been able to make all of its payments over the term of the mortgage.[111] The church paid it off in 1987.

Conditions had not improved by 1941. Records show that there were only eighty-three members, and there were only sixty-three baptisms recorded at Circular between 1912 and 1940. There was a spike in attendance during World War II, but that was temporary, due to military assignments in Charleston. Membership was approximately fifty in the 1950s. Only a few miscellaneous cosmetic renovations were made to the church over the years, the largest of which, done in 1941, was the broad platform steps that lead to the chancel.

By 1957, things seemed to be improving somewhat as Rev. Archie Bedford, in a resignation letter to the congregation, stated that he felt that his goal of "returning the church to its former strength" was partially complete as finances and membership had improved, but his language was cautiously optimistic. In 1966, a letter went out to members calling a special meeting to explore the financial condition of the church and "possible special money-making projects." In 1967, a letter pleading for help asked people to increase their pledges as they were running in the "red."

A further indicator of the problems of the congregation could be seen when Rev. Bob Boston began as pastor in 1968. He wrote a letter to the congregation just before he was to become pastor of Circular, listing reasons that members had related to him why the church would probably close. These included a building that was in dire need of repair, a small membership and members who had moved to the suburbs and found it difficult to come back into town to worship.

Rev. Boston was sent to Charleston by the United Presbyterian Church (UPC) to open a church. At the same time, Circular Church had very few members and was barely hanging on financially. Circular Church and the UPC entered into a mutually beneficial agreement that allowed Rev. Boston to become pastor of Circular. The UPC didn't have to build a new church, and Circular got a new minister whose salary was paid by the UPC for at least several years. During Rev. Boston's tenure at Circular, he helped the church revitalize itself by defining a new vision and finding its voice in the community. He served until 1974, when the Rev. Bert Keller became a part-time supply

Interior of sanctuary, showing steps added in 1941. *Courtesy Natalie Simpson.*

minister and, later, pastor. Rev. Keller would continue the vision of community service developed under Rev. Boston, and membership would grow steadily.

Rev. Keller came to Circular after he had done his master's work at Yale Divinity School and taught for three years at the Protestant Theological Seminary in Kisangani, Republic of the Congo. In 1969 he went into campus ministry in Charleston, and in 1974 he accepted the invitation to teach ethics on the faculty of the College of Medicine at the Medical University of South Carolina in Charleston. A few years after joining Circular, Rev. Keller became pastor. In recent years he completed a doctorate of ministry program at Princeton.

During Rev. Keller's tenure, the church has subscribed to the "tent-making ministry" theory that the apostle Paul practiced because he didn't want to be a burden on fledgling churches. That is, the minister straddles two worlds by having one foot in the church and one foot in the secular world through employment there. Paul was a tent maker as well as an apostle. The success of this type of ministry depends on a congregation being committed to an added level of activity. Circular's members have accepted this challenge. Nine half-time ministers have worked with Rev. Keller during his tenure: Peter Jorgensen (1973–75), Mark Deaton (1975–85), David Blackshear (1986–88), Susan Bouder (1988–90), Susan Hull (1991–94), Annette Nielsen (1995–98) and Susan Dunn (1990–91, 1994–95 and 1999–present).

One of these part-time ministers, Susan Dunn, has been with Circular for twenty-five years as a member and has served as lay minister for ten years of that time. She has served the church in a variety of ways, including her most recent project of helping make the new addition happen. She is an attorney in private practice. A native of Kentucky, Ms. Dunn graduated from Duke University and University of North Carolina–Chapel Hill, School of Law. She has over twenty years of experience as a mediator and has recently expanded her practice to include arbitration. She was one of the plaintiff's attorneys in *Ferguson v. City of Charleston*. This groundbreaking, constitutional case addressed Fourth Amendment issues relating to the drug testing of pregnant women. Her clients were victorious before the U.S. Supreme Court and ultimately settled the case.

By 1980, music again became the catalyst for action at the church, as it had been in 1930. By the 1980s, there was only a small church choir with an old electronic organ. The 1931 pipe organ, by that time, had fallen into disrepair, another sign of a struggling congregation. In the mid-1980s, Mr. Vernon Elliott was hired as Circular's church organist and sexton. As JoAnne Marcell, a longtime member of the present choir, writes:

> *Vernon could do almost anything, but he could not bring himself to play that old electronic organ. He rehearsed the choir using the piano and introduced interesting music that required no accompaniment. Recognizing the acoustic advantage of singing from the balcony, Vernon relocated the choir from the front of the church. The choir grew in numbers and quality of sound.*
>
> *Vernon's vision was that of having a working pipe organ again in the sanctuary. He located an exceptional Tracker organ, built for a church in Boston in 1890 by George S. Hutchings. Vernon preserved and relocated the case and pipes of the organ purchased in 1930 to their present site in the balcony, which made the windows in the sanctuary once again visible. He rebuilt the newly purchased Hutchings organ in the balcony. In 1998 Circular received a posthumous donation from Vernon Elliott to be kept in reserve for organ repair. The organ is called the Vernon Elliott Pipe Organ in memory of his immense contribution to Circular's music program. It is still in use today.*

By the mid-1980s, extensive renovations were needed, as the building had undergone no major renovations in almost a century. The congregation was small and money was short, so volunteers undertook a labor of love in order to preserve Circular's beautiful woodwork. Circular member Jim Dyke assumed the arduous task of erecting scaffolding to give access to the intricately curved support beams in the dome of the sanctuary, and then stripped the wood down to its original finish. Vernon Elliott stripped

Photo of sanctuary with organ purchased in 1930 blocking the windows. *Courtesy Elaine Simpson*.

1890 Hutchings Tracker organ purchased in Boston in the 1980s. *Courtesy Natalie Simpson*.

Organ pipes.

Hutchings label on organ. *Both photographs courtesy Natalie Simpson.*

Above: Organ keyboard.

Right: Scrollwork in balcony stripped by "Circular strippers." *Both photographs courtesy Natalie Simpson.*

Stained-glass window and woodwork.

Interior sanctuary and pews. *Both photographs courtesy Natalie Simpson.*

Quilt dedicated to Rev. Keller and hanging in Keller Hall. *Courtesy Mary Jane Ogawa, Jan Goin.*

the woodwork around the perimeter of the sanctuary and the large roll-up doors that separate the fellowship hall from the sanctuary. He was assisted by a group of members calling itself the "Circular strippers." They stripped all of the wood by hand, taking it back to its original finish. About a decade later the "strippers" were called back into action to strip the woodwork in the fellowship hall. The Building and Grounds Mission Group, formerly called committee, expanded the project by replacing the lighting in the room, repainting the walls and ceilings and refinishing the floor. The room was then dedicated in honor of the pastor, Rev. Bert Keller, and was named Keller Hall. Later, in 1999, a quilt was designed and executed by church members and presented to the church in honor of Rev. Keller. It is a rose medallion design copied from one of the church windows, and it hangs in Keller Hall.

In 1983 the Historic Charleston Foundation, a U.S. Department of Interior Grant, an IBM grant, local businessmen and Circular provided $50,000 for major graveyard restoration work. The project mapped the graveyard and catalogued more than five hundred tombstones, crypts, headstones and footstones. Restoration was done on graves from the colonial period. Many of these gravestones had sunk into the sandy soil over the years, and others had been misplaced in neighboring crypts and under the steps of the church. Earthquakes, fire, flood, heat and vandalism had taken their toll. The restoration was completed in 1985. Another round of building repairs was necessitated by Hurricane Hugo in 1989. Trees, tombstones and both buildings needed repairs.

SOCIAL CHANGES

As a Dissenter church Circular has, since its founding, regarded freedom of choice as essential. Founding members came to this country to guarantee their religious freedom. They challenged the Lords Proprietors and took their case to Parliament to win the right to choose their religion without losing their political rights. Their descendants were leaders in a revolution to found a country based on religious and political freedom. Throughout the church's history, members supported the rights of fellow members to leave and found their own church. They fought the Civil War in an attempt to maintain their own way of life. At the same time, there is evidence that they were conflicted by the fact that they were denying freedom to others. This conflict between living in society and living according to Christian principles has been a challenge faced by church members since 1681, and it makes for interesting reading in this chapter of church history. The first challenge was over women's rights.

Benjamin Hawes, 1781. The grave had sunk down into the sandy soil and was reset during the graveyard restorations. *Courtesy Natalie Simpson* (A2).

Steeple with scaffolding for repairs after Hugo. *Courtesy Ron Rocz.*

Harriet Theus, 1817, stone on brick base; additional damage done by Hugo.

Hurricane Hugo damaged stones, as seen by this fallen pillar and broken slab. *Both photographs courtesy CCGR* (B).

Above: Major Simeon Theus, 1821; this stone was damaged in Hurricane Hugo by a tree that fell against the pillar and knocked off the Theus urn (far right). At right is the grave of Susan Theus, 1856, and a tree that was blown over.

Right: Urn replaced after Hurricane Hugo. *Both photographs courtesy CCGR* (B).

Repaired urn, pillar and flat slab on left after Hugo.
Courtesy Natalie Simpson (B).

Role of Women

Major social changes of the twentieth century were beginning, with women leading the way. The history of Circular Church reflected that of society in that it was governed for most of its history almost exclusively by its white, male members. During the early years, the official presence of women in the church was largely overlooked, except when contributions were needed. This changed a bit with the founding of the early Ladies' Home Missionary Society in 1816 in that they were a recognized, organized group.

The next sign of change in the women's role in the church comes almost a century later in January of 1915. At the annual meeting, which only voting members could attend, and at which decisions for running the church for the next year were made, a letter was received from Miss Charlotte E. Lance, requesting that "a plain and full account from all sources of income, also from all of the various institutions of the church, with a full and plain account of all disbursement of the same, be printed or typewritten and sent to every member of the Church, that all may take an intelligent and vital interest in the Church and its affairs. This to be made a rule by the Corporation."[112] She was, in essence, proposing that the governance details of the church be made open to all.

These letters put in motion what proved to be an overturn of the official setup of the church. In July of 1915, changes were proposed in the constitution that made every communing member of the church over age twenty-one a member of the corporation, leaving out the word "male." The enfranchisement of the women of the church was the main object of the "bloodless revolution" that took place. "The time had passed when a little group of men, devoted and honest no doubt, could for a generation or two, with narrow and legalistic mind, control and really hinder the spiritual growth of the church."[113]

In 1917, at the semiannual meeting of voting members of the church, the presence of ladies is recorded for the first time in the history of the church. There were seven, together with nine men. A yard committee of three ladies was appointed: Charlotte Lance, Annie Graham and Mrs. W.H. Harvey. Since that time, ladies have served in a variety of capacities over the years. In 1927, Gertrude Thompson became the church treasurer. Kaye Sharpe was the first woman in the Clergy Society. The first female president of the church council was Bernadette Rowley in 1975. Since 1975, many women have served as president, and since 1993 the council presidency has alternated regularly between men and women.

Racial Integration

The next challenge faced by Circular during this era was that of racial integration. True to its Dissenter roots, in 1965, even before the United Church of Christ (UCC) took a stand on the issue, the congregation felt compelled by conscience to take a vote on whether to open the church to African Americans.

Integrating the most segregated institutions in America, its churches, has been a slow and difficult process for this country. During the 1960s and '70s, most Southern churches were having problems as they began to work through this issue. At some, the reaction to integration was simply to post people at the doors to keep blacks out. At Circular, members were not so united about the issue, and they went through a painful decision-making process.

The following information was taken from conversations recorded on tape during the "Conversations in Faith" oral history series recorded at Circular in the 1990s, and from letters from Bill and Kaye Sharpe written in the 1960s. From them we get a clear picture of what the decision-making process was like.

Circular's pastor, Rev. William Barnhart, was opposed to integrating the church. No one believed that he was a racist, but most felt that he did not wish to integrate the church because of fear of damage to the church by those opposed to integration, especially to the stained-glass windows. He presented three arguments against integrating: (1) This is not the time. Other institutions such as schools and city governments are not yet integrated. (2) Nothing can be done except through the power structure. (3) The church will lose members if it has an open-door policy.

The final count, which was very close, was negative toward integrating the church. Members have since stated that they felt this vote was the result of a desire to be loyal to their pastor, Rev. Barnhart.[114] The decision was not to stand, however. After the vote, the president of the council, Bill Sharpe, resigned. In his impassioned letter of resignation he said that he could

> *no longer serve as head of a church that denies the brotherhood of man. How un-Christian can we get…Our Church is split right down the middle on the race issue, an issue that won't go away. If we are to remain an effective church this issue has to be resolved. We cannot hide from it. We cannot sweep it under the rug. As a church we have been split for months but have refused to face the fact and have refused to discuss it openly with those who disagree with us. We gather around and discuss it with those who agree with our way of thinking, thus widening the split…*
>
> *Let no one interpret this resignation as a sign of weakness. I intend to work to the best of my ability to have an open door policy at Circular Church. I resigned as a protest to the segregated policy voted by our congregation. I resigned also to bring this issue to a head so that we can resolve it and once again make the church an effective force in the community.*

Kaye Sharpe then sent a letter to the church treasurer stating that she and her husband would not be able to support the church financially any more, as they had long had a personal policy of not supporting businesses that practiced segregation. They felt that they could certainly not support a church that did so. The letter outlined their belief that the church should be leading the way instead of following, that waiting for the power structure denied the importance Jesus placed upon the individual and that the power structure would only be moved by hundreds of little people taking a stand.

Several weeks later another vote was taken and the result was in favor of integrating Circular. The vote was by a large majority, some think unanimous (although on the tape Kaye Sharp expressed her opinion that nothing at Circular is ever unanimous). After the open-door policy was ratified, however, a number of people left the church.[115]

There was not a huge flow of African American members into Circular as a result of the vote. During the 1950s and '60s, Circular members and members of Plymouth Congregational Church worshipped together on Sunday evenings. Occasionally, Circular had black visitors, but there were no black members at the time, or for some time after.[116] Today the congregation is much more integrated, but not to the degree hoped for in the '60s.

One notable African American member of the church, who joined several years before her death in 2003 at the age of 101, was Ruby Cornwell. She was influential in Charleston as a civil rights activist and member of the board of the NAACP. Her obituary in the *Post and Courier* relates a famous incident when she was arrested in a 1960s sit-in at an elegant Charleston restaurant. She wore a white silk dress, hat and gloves, and was treated apologetically by the arresting officer. She was proud of her "record," and said that she had always "raised quiet, refined hell." She helped found the MOJA festival and was a board member of the Carolina Art Association, which governs the Gibbes Museum of Art. Her presence and sense of style brought a continuing awareness of the importance of keeping racial issues before the congregation.

In a continuing effort to increase Circular's commitment toward racial justice, Circular Church entered into a partnership with Morris Brown AME Church. Members from the two churches meet monthly and discuss ways to further interracial dialogue. The partnership has sponsored a mentoring and a tutoring group at Burke High School since 2003. Jack Quigley, who came to Circular after retiring in Charleston, further invigorated the group in 2004 by partnering with Delores Jones of Morris Brown AME to develop a Dismantling Racism Retreat between the two churches and to form several dialogue groups to discuss racism, its causes and its effects.

Nuclear Freeze

In the 1980s, Circular was faced with another decision on a very controversial national and local issue. The church went through a process of self-examination, this time to determine how it should react to the arms race within the context of being Christian. In 1983, the General Assembly of the United Presbyterian Church, with which the church was affiliated, asked all of its congregations to endorse the nuclear freeze amendment. This was the height of the Cold War. Both the United States and the Soviet Union were building nuclear weapons. The world was becoming involved in a runaway arms race. In Charleston, which had one of the biggest military complexes on the East Coast, including the largest submarine base in the world, the issue was extremely controversial.

Circular was divided on the issue. A commander of a nuclear submarine was a member of the congregation, as were his wife and several other military families. Others in the congregation were members of the Palmetto Alliance, a peace organization. The church took this opportunity to discuss one of the most pressing social subjects of our time, holding a series of meetings and films leading up to the vote on the issue. Feelings were high on both sides, and both sides had excellent arguments. The vote was seventy to twelve endorsing the nuclear freeze. The most remarkable thing about the process was that no one left the church over the issue, probably because the arguments on both sides had been respected. Over time, Circular took a visible public stance on the issue. As the pastor, Bert Keller, put it, "The peacemaking ministry, including explicit worship services, preaching, media statements, dialogue, resolutions, and demonstrating by the tracks that the White Train used to bring nuclear armaments into the Naval Weapons Station, was a defining part of the church in the '80s." Circular's Dissenter roots were showing again.

An Open and Affirming Church: Case Study of Defining Identity
The third major decision on a social issue made by church members in the late twentieth century was that of becoming an "open and affirming church." The following is a review of that process written by the current pastor, Bert Keller.

The Circular congregation became aware of active participation of gay and lesbian members and friends when the issue of homosexuality came "out of the closet" in the 1980s. Before that decade, homosexuality was not part of the congregation's consciousness and gay and lesbian individuals and couples were treated like everybody else without comment.

In October 1981, a congregation of the Metropolitan Community Church (MCC) was organized in Charleston. The new group approached Circular for permission to use the church's space for worship, having been turned down by another church in the city. Rather than simply acting on the request, council perceived it as an opportunity to involve the entire congregation in a decision-making process that would serve to clarify the church's position regarding homosexuality and Christian faith. A three-week study program was developed to involve as many members as possible in a substantive discussion of the issue, resulting in a congregational meeting to approve or disapprove hosting the MCC.

The process succeeded in exploring biblically and theologically how Circular should approach the question. After a month of dialogue, the congregational vote was roughly sixty to ten in favor of inviting the MCC to use the sanctuary for worship. One Circular family discontinued their giving to the church for the period that the MCC was using the facility. Circular's accepting posture toward persons of same-sex orientation became part of the identity of the church.

A few years later, in 1985, the United Church of Christ adopted its Open and Affirming (ONA) policy in General Synod and requested its constituent congregations to study the matter, write their own Open and Affirming Statements and formally adopt them. Circular responded to that challenge as a further opportunity to clarify and broadcast the church's position on inclusiveness and sexual orientation. Council authorized a task force to carry out the process and bring a report to the membership. Opportunity was given for misgivings to be expressed and dissenting opinions heard. The point was made forcefully that "open and affirming" does not mean mere "toleration," but that gay and lesbian persons are affirmed in their loving relationships and lifestyle for who they are and because they bring value to the community gathered in Christ's name. The final draft was presented for discussion by the congregation a month in advance of the Annual Meeting. Circular's Open and Affirming Statement was presented and brought to a vote in an attitude of prayer. The vote of the Annual Meeting was seventy to zero in favor of adoption.

OUTREACH MINISTRY

The church bulletin reminds us weekly that "each member of Circular Church is engaged in ministry—each uses his or her talents to serve others, to build up the whole church community, and to work for justice and human dignity in all aspects of life." Members of Circular have demonstrated their commitment to this principle by their outreach into the community and the wider world stage.

One of the earliest documented instances of charitable giving from records of this period of church history is that of giving to the survivors of the Galveston Hurricane of 1900, the deadliest disaster in American history to that date, and to the victims of the San Francisco earthquake of 1906, which killed between 450 and 700 people.[117] Having been pounded by many hurricanes and having lost their church to fire in 1861 and earthquake in 1886, Circular Church members must have felt a deep connection to the victims of these two events.

In 1917, a program of social service for the men of the army and navy under the direction of Miss Ruth Graham, sponsored by the Ladies' Missionary Society, was begun in the early summer. The lower floor of Lance Hall was the first space in the city to be opened for this purpose. It was used from 1:00 p.m. to 9:00 p.m. as a recreational and writing center, then also a reading center.

During World War II, Charleston's population greatly increased; additional responsibilities were met by a broad program of hospitality to servicemen and -women. Special socials and services were held for soldiers and sailors on Thursday and Sunday evenings. The War Victims and Service Committee of the denomination cooperated with the church in providing an assistant to the pastor. A special project was carried on at Dorchester Terrace, a new settlement near the Charleston Navy Yard. A

Lance Hall, 1859, rebuilt in 1867 and 1886 to house the congregation until the current sanctuary was erected. Lance Hall is the first floor, named after Charlotte Lance. The second floor was named for Ruth Graham. *Courtesy Natalie Simpson.*

Sunday school of about fifty was organized there, and pastoral work was done among resident families.[118]

During the late '60s, the '70s and much of the '80s, Circular seemed to undergo a rejuvenation. Rev. Bob Boston, who became pastor in 1968, would breathe new life into Circular by encouraging its members to look outside of themselves by serving the community. This was a period of social unrest in America, including Charleston. When hippies were prevented by police from gathering in large numbers on King Street, Circular, under the guidance of Rev. Boston, invited them to gather at Lance Hall, despite their dirt, noise and long hair. They were also welcomed to worship. Circular was one of the few places these folks felt welcome in Charleston. As they gathered here, the problems of alienated youngsters, runaways, their parents and the drug culture became visible. Homeless people were found sleeping in the graveyard, some in the unsealed vaults.

Under Rev. Boston's leadership, Circular became a catalyst, not only for those in trouble, but also for groups that were attempting to serve their needs. Space was given in Lance Hall to help groups who needed space to get started, and frequently the church contributed funds as well. Circular took on an active role in identifying needs in the community and trying to meet these needs either directly or by connecting with other agencies

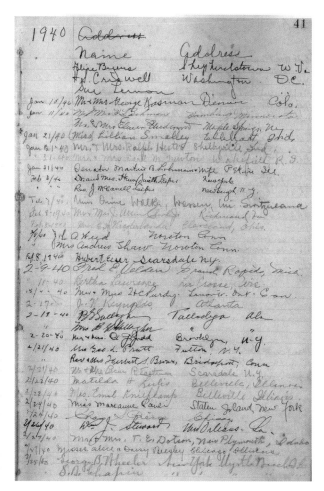

1940 visitor's record illustrating the number of out-of-town guests and tourists attending Circular weekly. Visitors were even more numerous in the war years because of the military bases in Charleston. *Courtesy South Carolina Historical Society.*

and churches in the city. Either in or through Circular Church, Bread for Life, Crisis Ministries, Hospice of Charleston, Elder Shelter, Amnesty International, Charleston PEACE, Inter-Faith Crisis Ministry, Nuclear Freeze Campaign, Alcoholics Anonymous, Narcotics Anonymous, Parents without Partners, People against Rape and My Sister's House were started in Charleston. Rev. Boston also began a Marriage and Family Counseling Center in Lance Hall. This was a pioneering effort, and hundreds were served. In 1974, he resigned as pastor of Circular to become a full-time director of this center where people in trouble found a nonjudgmental and supportive place.

In addition to giving church space to aid community organizations, members have worked on or contributed money to a wide range of projects ranging from giving to organizations around the world to meeting many local

Peace Pole erected in the 1980s as part of an international peace effort. *Courtesy Natalie Simpson* (A1/B).

needs. Currently, the Global and Community Ministries Group oversees the church's giving to local and global projects. The Circular Church Mission Fund gives to members who desire to start up a project that would benefit the local community, would include other members of the church in its implementation and would be self-sufficient after the first year. Recipients must go through a grant process. This fund, for example, helped to start the safe drinking water project for families in the Seewee to Santee area, which led to a large federal/state grant to the area for improved water supply.

Another type of outreach work began a tradition of mission trips for youth and adults. As part of the confirmation classes held every two years, youth ages twelve to fourteen are encouraged to spend a week together doing work to help those less fortunate than themselves. Since 1998, groups have gone to Tijuana, Mexico; Princeville, North Carolina; Juarez, Mexico (twice); and Biloxi, Mississippi, to repair or build homes.

Concern for the schools of Charleston has led to two recent efforts in community schools. In 1996, Circular Church entered into an "adoption" with James Simmons Elementary School. Since that time, members of Circular have acted as mentors and tutors there, and the Environmental Group has taken students on field trips to increase student awareness of and interaction with the environment of the Lowcountry. In 2002, Circular began a mentoring and tutoring program at Burke High School in conjunction with Morris Brown AME Church.

Crisis Ministry, 573 Meeting Street. *Courtesy Paul Calhoun.*

In the mid-1990s, the deacons organized caretaking efforts of the church into a network that communicates well and responds to needs in a variety of ways. The network is meant to support members and friends of Circular in times of crisis or particular need. Most often support is shown by providing meals when there is a birth, a death or a hospitalization in a family. Small groups of members are organized into "tribes," like the twelve tribes of Israel. When a need arises within a tribe, its Pastoral Care Associate recruits members of the tribe to help out. If the need is greater than one tribe can meet, the entire church is invited to volunteer to help.

THE "GREEN" BUILDING

One of the issues still testing the congregation today is how we fit into the natural environment while making the smallest "footprint," or causing the least damage. Circular's need for increased space, studied for years, became a test of the congregation's commitment to put environmental beliefs into action. In 2007, the members of Circular dedicated their first new building in more than a century. In its own way it drew as much attention and required as much effort as the much larger buildings in its history. The building is an addition to Lance Hall, the Sunday school and meeting facility that was built in 1859. The building is, additionally,

Circular Mission Group in Juarez, Mexico. *Courtesy Elaine Simpson.*

"green." At a time when global warming and climate change are drawing much discussion, the building is one of the most energy-efficient in the Lowcountry. It utilizes a roof garden, a geothermal heating and cooling system, a rainwater-collecting system and a passive-solar design.

Construction was not easily completed, nor was it inexpensive. The building was the climax of a process that took more than seven years to complete. Frank Harmon, of Raleigh, North Carolina, nationally known for his energy-efficient designs, was chosen as the architect. The available land for construction was part of the church's graveyard; thus, considerable work was necessary to move both graves and gravestones. Fundraising was crucial as the building itself was costly, and renovations to Lance Hall added to the total. However, as the plans were displayed, members responded enthusiastically, and eventually more than $1.2 million was raised and a mortgage was taken out for the remaining costs. The higher than usual costs for the eco-friendly building should be offset by dramatically lower operating costs.

The result is a building that doesn't just accommodate the needs of the growing congregation; the structure is a beautiful evocation of the church's environmental ethic and, according to Charleston Mayor Joe Riley's speech at the dedication, an inspiration to others in the community. Locally available building materials were used whenever possible to reduce pollution during transportation. The geothermal heating and cooling system should

Above: These graves were moved because of a new addition to Lance Hall (A1).

Right: More graves moved to front of the church on Meeting Street. *Both photographs courtesy Natalie Simpson* (A1).

Left: Pillar and graves moved to front of church because of new addition to Lance Hall. (A1).

Below: New addition to Lance Hall. *Both photographs courtesy Natalie Simpson.*

Right: Entry to second floor of Lance Hall from the new addition.

Below: Glass wall in the new addition. *Both photographs courtesy Natalie Simpson.*

View of neighboring office building, sanctuary and Lance Hall from the new addition.

Floor plaque in new addition marking the spot where Grimball family members were buried in the 1840s. It is embedded over the burial spot. *Both photographs courtesy Natalie Simpson.*

Mayor Joseph Riley speaking at the dedication of the new addition to Lance Hall.

Children burying time capsule at dedication of the new building. *Both photographs courtesy Mike Marcell.*

"Into the Light" quilt made for the kickoff of the Capital Campaign to raise money for repairs and for the new building. *Courtesy Paul Calhoun.*

save 30 to 40 percent on monthly energy costs. The roof garden lowers peak roof temperatures from the normal 150 degrees to about 90 degrees. The green elevator, crucial for accessibility, uses 75 percent less energy than conventional styles and generates its own electricity while descending. The passive design provides shade in the summer and direct sunlight in the winter. The two-thousand-gallon rainwater collection cistern provides water for landscape use.

Members are gradually realizing the bonuses: open porches wide enough to hold classes, a secluded courtyard that invites meditation, the satisfaction of knowing that the roof garden will absorb carbon dioxide and release oxygen, thereby fighting global warming, and the pride of helping set the standard for green architecture in the Lowcountry.

SUMMARY

Today, the majority of Circular's congregation is no longer made up of the descendants of its original founders. Some members are still native South Carolinians, but many come from other parts of the country. Much like the church's founders, they are businessmen, professionals, artisans, doctors, political activists, lawyers, fishermen, gardeners, teachers and writers. Many still live on the Charleston peninsula; most travel to work daily on streets

Rev. Bert Keller, pastor of Circular Congregational Church from 1974 to the present. *Courtesy Lucille Keller.*

Some twentieth-century member donations to the church. The cross was donated in memory of Mrs. Agnes Kessler, the ceramic communion service was made and donated by Rose Mitchell and the carpet was donated by members celebrating their wedding anniversary. *Courtesy Natalie Simpson.*

Above: Ernest and Barbara Wingard, longtime members of Circular.

Right: Kaye and Bill Sharpe, longtime members of Circular. *Both photographs courtesy Paul Calhoun.*

that are named for founding members. Several live on Sol Legare Island. Some come from the suburban areas that were once plantations owned by members. While modern medicine has eliminated the pestilences suffered by early congregations, today's congregation still faces hurricanes and heat, still continues to face monetary problems and still struggles to maintain a balance between material and spiritual.

Special mention should be made here of the Sharpes and the Wingards, who have been members of our congregation for more than fifty years. Barbara Wingard was baptized at Circular and her relatives have been leaders throughout the history of the present church. Ernest was treasurer for twenty-six years and both were members of the Clergy Society. Kaye and Bill Sharpe have each served as council president, both have been members of the Clergy Society and together they led the church to an open-door policy of integration.

Since Rev. Keller has been pastor at Circular for thirty-three years, it seems fitting that his words should summarize the present section of Circular's history. Of his tenure here he says,

> *During this period, American religion has taken a decided turn to the right, and many churches that have not followed suit have declined in numbers and influence. Circular has countered both trends. The congregation has consistently defined itself in terms of a passionate spiritual search for truth, non-dogmatic theology rich in metaphor, affirmation of persons regardless of race or sexual orientation, and public action for peace, economic justice, and environmental integrity.*

5.

INTRODUCTION TO THE CIRCULAR CHURCH GRAVEYARD

Information compiled by Pat Spaulding
Archivist of Circular Congregational Church

The graveyard of the Circular Congregational Church, in use since about 1690, is one of the oldest burial grounds in Charleston. These tombstones can provide genealogists with a wealth of information on Lowcountry families. More than 150 gravestones currently found in the churchyard predate the Revolutionary War. There are over 450 names of people buried there who were born before 1800. Fewer than 100 individuals were buried between 1860 and 1900, and only about 30 more have been buried there in the twentieth century.

There are around 730 individuals named on just over 500 stones identified in the yard. In addition, there are over 350 burial records found in a list of "Probable Burials" and 275 more records considered "Possible Burials." That makes a total of more than 1,350 recorded burials. It is thought that by 1860, there had been over 5,000 burials in the Circular churchyard, in an area that seemed capable of holding about 1,000 bodies. Recent excavations necessitated by the new addition to Lance Hall confirm these estimates.[119]

No doubt many of the earliest records have been lost. In 1905 there was a fairly systematic recording of inscriptions that existed at the time. Some of the inscriptions were illegible then, and more have become illegible in the intervening years. A recent effort at recording all existing burial records was made in order to preserve for future generations the names and last memorials of those who once worshipped with the oldest dissenting church in South Carolina.

In her book *Early Gravestone Art in Georgia and South Carolina*, which focused on stones of "iconic or imagistic significance" (those with engraved

Graveyard with oak. *Courtesy Natalie Simpson.*

pictures), Diana W. Combs identifies many of our early slate stones as an "extraordinary and irreplaceable legacy of our artistic and cultural past." She further states that the Circular Congregational Church in Charleston is the "richest repository of eighteenth-century iconic gravestones in the country."

In *The Buildings of Charleston—A Guide to the City's Architecture,* Jonathan H. Poston states, "More than fifty slate stones imported from New England constitute the largest concentration of the work of Boston and Rhode Island carvers in the Southeast." Mould and Loewe's *Historic Gravestone Art of Charleston, South Carolina, 1695–1802* surmises that the "quality and variety of early funerary art in the Circular churchyard can be attributed to the diversity of its founding worshipers," who were Dissenters. They were primarily French, Scots, English or they were from New England. "Their relationships with family members, friends and business associates in Massachusetts, Rhode Island, Connecticut and other northern colonies undoubtedly helped bring the work of New England's gravestone-makers to Charleston." Their diversity perhaps accounted for the Southern church members' desire for more ornate and fashionable stones than those of the more puritanical New England customers of the stone carvers.

Books detailing burial records of Circular Church's graveyard can be found in the church office, in the South Carolina Historical Society collection, at the Charleston County Public Library and the Library Society. They are listed alphabetically by family name within three categories: Currently Existing Stones, Probable Burials and Possible Burials.

CURRENTLY EXISTING STONES

The book *Graveyard Burials 1695–1995 of the Independent or Congregational Church of Charleston*, compiled by Pat Spaulding, includes those 730 individuals whose burials are recorded as part of the inscription of a currently existing stone. See inscriptions in binders in church office for graveyard sections A, B, C and D. In addition to the inscriptions, there may be a photograph of the stone, comments about the family and notes about the gravestone art or carvers. Maps and instructions on finding a stone in the graveyard are also provided.

PROBABLE BURIALS (NO STONES EXIST), 1732–1897

The 352 names in the "Probable" section of the book were discovered in church records but no stones have been found for them. Sources of the records are:

1. Church Records, *South Carolina Historical and Genealogical Magazine (SCHGM)* (1732–1738)
2. Death Notices, *South Carolina Gazette* (1732–1774)
3. William Hutson Register, *SCHGM* (1756–1760)
4. Isaac Hayne Records, *SCHGM* (1764–1780)
5. Benjamin Palmer Records, Circular Church Archives (1815–1836)
6. Other Burial Records from Miscellaneous Sources, Circular Church Archives (1776–1841, 1844–1897)

POSSIBLE BURIALS (NO STONES EXIST), 1815–1836

The 275 names in the "Possible" section were also found in early church records. There is reason to believe they <u>may</u> have been buried in the yard, but some doubt exists. The source of the records is *Dr. Benjamin Palmer's Funeral Record Book from 1815–1836.*

Right: Nathan Bassett, 1738. Only known work by Willliam Codner that is signed, and also the oldest portrait stone found anywhere in America. (A2).

Below: Elizabeth Simmons, 1740. "H EMMES BOSTON" signature. *Both photographs courtesy Missy Loewe* (A1).

Solomon Milner, 1757. (B).

David Stoddard, 1760. *Both photographs courtesy Missy Loewe* (B).

Signature of stonecutter Lemuel Savery, "Leml. Savery fecit Plimo, N.E." (Lemuel Savery made it, Plymouth, New England.) This is believed to be the only signed stone by Savery. (A2).

Bottom of gravestone of the Rev. Nathan Bassett, 1738. Only known signed Codner gravestone: "Wm. Codner Boston, N.E." *Both photographs courtesy Natalie Simpson* (A2).

UNIQUE STONES

1. The first portrait on an American grave (and only known signed stone by William Codner, a Boston artisan of unusual skills and adaptability) adorns the 1738 stone of Rev. Nathan Bassett, which predates the first portrait stone in New England by six years.

2. The finest baroque slate gravestone still intact from the colonial period[120] is that of Elizabeth Simmons, 1740.

3. The most notable and best preserved example of neoclassicism from eighteenth-century Charleston[121] is Solomon Milner's stone, 1757.

4. The only existing example in the Southeast of a death's head and a soul figure on the same marker[122] appears on David Stoddard's grave, 1760.

NOTED STONE CARVERS' SOLE SIGNATURES AT CIRCULAR

1. The only known signed gravestone by Lemuel Savery of Plymouth, New England, is that of Benjamin Hawes, 1781.

2. Rev. Nathan Bassett's stone is the only known signed stone by William Codner of Boston.

3. A potential sole signature is on the Thomas Lamboll stone, signed by a carver from Stratford-on-Avon, England. This stone used an urn as its centerpiece twenty years before the image became common on gravestones in America. The signature appears as "W. Vere Fec't Stratford Essex. (See "Together Forever" section that follows.)

RARE SIGNATURES

1. John Bull on the graves of the Savage brothers.

2. George Allen ("G Allen sculp") on the graves of Mary Smith and Charles Warham.

3. George Allen or his brother Gabriel ("G Allen Sc. Pro. Rhode Island") on the grave of Dr. Richard Savage.

4. Henry Emmes signed "H EMMES BOSTON" on the graves of Elizabeth Simmons, the Honorable Isaac Holmes and Solomon Milner.

5. Lamson family stones were never signed, but Circular has the only known stones in town, or possibly in the entire Southern United States.

Top of three Savage brothers' crypt. The three cherubs (*putti* figures) represent the brothers. One holds a rope that the others seem to be trying to hold onto, perhaps to stay together in death. (B).

Signature of George Allen Jr. of Rehobeth, Rhode Island, at the bottom of the gravestone of Mary Smith, 1795. *Both photographs courtesy Natalie Simpson* (B).

Charles Warham, 1779, with George Allen signature. *Courtesy Daniel Farber* (B).

Dr. Richard Savage, 1789. *Courtesy CCGR* (B).

Detail from grave of Dr. Richard Savage, carved by George or Gabriel Allen. (B).

Dr. Richard Savage. Signature "G Allen Sc. Pro Rhode Island." *Both photographs courtesy Daniel Farber* (B).

Elizabeth Simmons, 1740. *Courtesy Natalie Simpson* (A1).

"Boston," part of signature of Henry Emmes on the bottom of Isaac Holmes's grave. *Courtesy Missy Loewe* (B).

Grave of Honorable Isaac Holmes, 1751. Notable for having both a portrait and a skull and crossbones and for lettering that is on a curved line rather than straight. There is a Henry Emmes signature on bottom. *Courtesy Natalie Simpson* (B).

Top of gravestone of Isaac Holmes, 1751. The portrait was damaged by flying debris during a tornado in 1939. *Courtesy Missy Loewe* (B).

Signature of Henry Emmes, "HEmmes Boston Fec (I made it)," on the bottom of the gravestone of Solomon Milner, 1751. *Courtesy Natalie Simpson* (B).

WHOSE TOMBSTONE IS IN THIS GRAVEYARD? A SAMPLING

1. Benjamin Hawes—coach maker who died during the British occupation of Charleston
2. Nathan Bassett—signed at the bottom by William Codner, Boston
3. Captain Clark—the ship and inscription on this obelisk indicate that this captain went down with his ship
4. John Clifford—butcher who acquired large portions of Vanderhorst lands in 1750, "was a loving Husband, a tender Parent & a sincere Friend"; he died "after a tedious illness"
5. Ann Dart—oldest dated grave marker in the city
6. Josiah Flagg—first American-born dentist
7. John Bee Holmes and Hon. John Edwards—Revolutionary Patriots buried in the same crypt
8. Hutson/Peronneau vault—holds grave of the first mayor (intendant) of Charleston
9. Lamboll family—an exceptional grouping of cherubs of differing wing designs
10. Mary Owen—slate portraiture stone that is representational; the portrait has a hat and Mary Owen was a milliner
11. Peronneau family—a large grouping of stones of one of the most prominent early families in South Carolina
12. Eleazer Phillips—first printer in Charleston

Top of Benjamin Hawes's, 1781, grave, showing an unusual combination of the soul effigy and the crossbones. The soul effigy is interesting for its long nose and pointy chin. *Courtesy Natalie Simpson* (B).

Nathan Bassett, 1738. *Courtesy Paul Calhoun* (A1/B).

Tomb of Captain Richard Clark, 1861; Captain Leslie, 1853; his wife, 1853; and two daughters, Martha and Anne, 1853. Captain Clark was left alone to grieve when the Leslie family went down together at sea. (C).

Storm-tossed ship carving on the tomb of Captain Clark and the Leslie family. *Both photographs courtesy Natalie Simpson* (C).

Above: John Clifford, 1764. *Courtesy CCGR* (B).

Below: Ann Dart, 1729, oldest grave marker in the city, *center of photo*; Mary, her sister, 1736, *right*, and a sibling (name unreadable), 1731, *left. Courtesy Natalie Simpson* (A1).

Memorial to Josiah Flagg, 1816, erected in the twentieth century. (B).

Grave of John Bee Holmes, 1827, and family members from the Holmes and Edwards families. John Bee Holmes married Elizabeth Edwards, daughter of John Edwards, a wealthy merchant and Revolutionary hero who died in exile in Philadelphia, leaving ten children. *Both photographs courtesy Natalie Simpson* (C).

The Hutson/Peronneau vault holds members of the Hutson and Peronneau families. Hutson descendants placed the memorial plaque on the west wall in 1995. A large tomb was a prestige symbol. (C).

Three Lamboll children: Benjamin, 1738, age ten months; Mary, 1740, age sixteen months; and Benjamin, 1742, age three months. To their right is the grave of their mother, Margaret, 1742. Her image looks down toward them. *Both photographs courtesy Natalie Simpson* (B).

Benjamin Lamboll, 1749. Note the unusually expressive cherub. *Courtesy CCGR* (B).

Grave of Mary Owen, 1749. *Courtesy Missy Loewe* (C).

Above: Sarah Peronneau, 1747. *Courtesy Daniel Farber.* (B).

Right: Eleazer Phillips, 1732, first printer in South Carolina. *Courtesy Missy Loewe* (B).

Above: Rev. Reuben Post, 1858, his wife Harriott, 1857, and their daughter, Frances, 1842. The gravestones are chess pieces—Rev. Post is the king, his wife the queen and Frances is the rook. (C).

Left: Nathaniel Russell, 1820. *Both photographs courtesy Natalie Simpson* (C).

Full view of Savage crypt. The signature at the bottom reads, "J Bull Engr(aver chipped off) Newport." *Courtesy Missy Loewe* (B).

Simmons Crypt containing Henry, 1695, and Frances, 1707. This is the oldest tomb structure in Charleston. *Courtesy CCGR* (A1).

13. Rev. Reuben Post and family—pastor's family stones were erected by the congregation in forms of king, queen and rook

14. Nathaniel Russell—extremely wealthy Charleston merchant whose home is now a house museum

15. Savage Crypt—marks the grave of three brothers who died within ten days of one another; carved by John Bull

16. Elizabeth Simmons—fine New England slate portrait by H. Emmes, Boston

17. Symonds crypt—the oldest surviving grave marker in Charleston

TOGETHER FOREVER

Above: May family graves. At right are Mary, 1877, and John, 1859, and three of their children: year-old twins Henry and Edward, 1823, and nine-year-old John, 1836. Brother James, 1873, is at left. (A1).

Right: Grave of Elizabeth Holmes, 1758, granddaughter of Archibald Stobo and wife of Isaac Holmes Jr. Her attire and her husband's on the next stone are quite fashionable in their detail. *Both photographs courtesy Natalie Simpson* (B).

161

Grave of Isaac Holmes Jr., 1763, grandson of Henry Peronneau, and his nine-month-old daughter, Susanna. His epitaph calls him "a tender Husband, an affectionate Parent, and indulgent Master & a sincere Christian." (B).

Pillar monument for Thomas Napier, 1860, and his wife, Rebekah Theus Napier, 1864. *Both photographs courtesy Natalie Simpson* (B).

Cradle grave of Anne Napier, 1858. (B).

Three vaults of the Mathewes family. Anthony Mathewes, 1735, in the middle, was a pew holder listed in 1732. *Both photographs courtesy Natalie Simpson* (B).

Tomb of Anthony Toomer, 1798, his wife Ann Warham Toomer, 1827, and son Charles, 1778. Toomer, a brick mason, was a major in the Revolutionary War and a member of the Sons of Liberty. *Courtesy Natalie Simpson* (B).

Rev. William Hutson, 1761, and his second wife, Mary, 1760. The grave of his first wife, also Mary, is on the other side of Rev. Hutson's grave. *Courtesy Missy Loewe* (B).

Above: Elizabeth Lamboll, 1770, noted horticulturist. (B).

Right: Thomas Lamboll, 1774, prominent judge who became involved in his wife's horticultural interests. *Both photographs courtesy CCGR* (B).

Interesting Details

Merchant David Stoddard, 1769, noted for the carvings of a toothy skull looking to the side, crossbones and a soul effigy. The stone was probably carved by John Homer of Boston. *Courtesy Natalie Simpson* (B).

George Heskett, 1747. Gravestone is noted for the detail of his clothing. He is wearing a multi-buttoned coat and fringed scarf. *Courtesy Missy Loewe* (B).

Rev. William Hutson, 1761. (B).

Top of Rev. William Hutson's gravestone with *putti* (singular "*putto*," a figure of a small child, sometimes unclothed) figures leaning on skull and hourglass. *Both photographs courtesy Natalie Simpson* (B).

Above: Top of grave of Mary Smith, 1795. The stone is noted for the detail of the weeping ladies' hands and handkerchiefs, as well as the flowing motion of their gowns. (B).

Below left: Susan Boswell Theus, 1856, relict of Simeon Theus. The fallen oak probably symbolizes a life cut short. (B).

Below right: Mary Lamboll, 1743. A classical bust image, she has piercing eyes, curled hair, a dimple on her chin and a long nose. Her dress is fashionably low cut. *All three photographs courtesy Natalie Simpson* (B).

Above: Crypt of three Savage brothers, 1784. Note the vandalism that turned "all" into "ah and "one" into "ohe" by scratching lines to alter words. *Courtesy Natalie Simpson* (B).

Below: Charles Warham, 1779. Stone noted for its exceptional winged angel detail. *Courtesy Daniel Farber* (B).

Appendix A

CIRCULAR CHURCH GRAVEYARD MAP

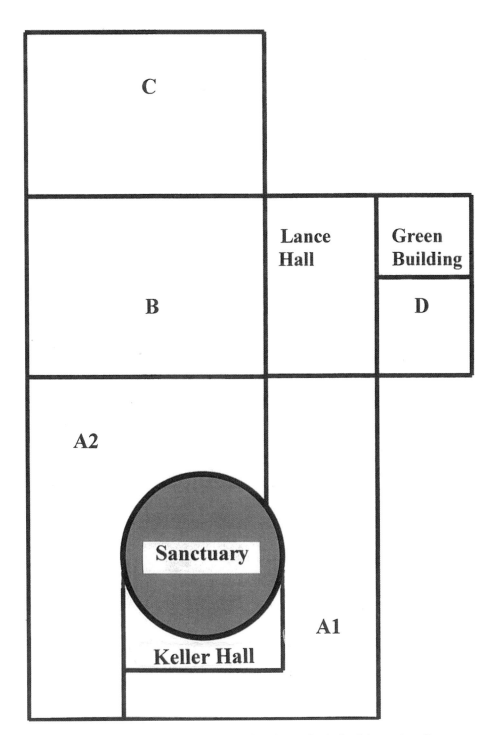

Map of Circular Graveyard, cross-referenced with pictures in the book by section. *Courtesy Lisa Hayes.*

Appendix B

MINISTERS

1681–1691: We have scant information about the early ministers of the first forty-foot-square meetinghouse of Charleston. In the publication of *American Presbyterianism: Its Origin and Early History*, author Charles A. Briggs refers to both Thomas Barrett and William Dunlop as being early missionaries settled in the Charleston area.

PASTORS	FROM*
1691: Benjamin Pierpont	Roxbury, Massachusetts
1698: Hugh Adams	Massachusetts
1698: John Cotton	Plymouth, Massachusetts
1700: Archibald Stobo	Scotland
1704: William Livingston	Ireland
1724: Nathan Bassett	Roxbury, Massachusetts
1734: Josiah Smith	Charleston, South Carolina
1740: James Parker	Gravesend, England
1753: James Edmonds	England
1756: William Hutson	England
1761: Andrew Bennett	England
1767: John Thomas	Wales
1772: William Tennent	Norwalk, Connecticut
1783: William Hollinshead	Fairfield, New Jersey
1788: Isaac S. Keith	Alexandria, Virginia
1814: Benjamin M. Palmer	Charleston, South Carolina
1815: Anthony Forster	North Carolina
1836: Reuben Post	Washington, D.C.
1859: Alonzo G. Fay	New York
1860: Thomas O. Rice	Brighton, Massachusetts
1867: William Hooper Adams	Boston, Massachusetts

1879: A.H. Missildine	Lebanon, Missouri
1888: Henry M. Grant	Middleboro, Massachusetts
1899: J. Edward Kirbye	Provo, Utah
1902: Augustus J. Davisson	Herndon, Virginia
1904: J. Sherman Calhoun	Forrest, Illinois
1906: Gardner S. Butler	Demorest, Georgia
1911: Benjamin Rush Thornberry	Somonauk, Illinois
1912: E. Cullum Grimshaw	Hammond, Louisiana
1915: A.S. Gaffney	Atlanta, Georgia
1917: George Evans Paddack	Tryon, North Carolina
1926: George N. Edwards	Walla Walla, Washington
1941: C. Rexford Raymond	Gates County, North Carolina
1951: Archie Bedford	Syracuse, New York
1958: William Barnhart	Frederick, Maryland
1968: Robert Boston	Darlington, South Carolina
1974: Albert Keller	Birmingham, Alabama

*The places of origin listed for the ministers are, at times, their place of birth and at times where they served before they came to our church, depending on available information.

Appendix C

CIRCULAR CHURCH TOUR MAP OF CHARLESTON

Peninsular Charleston

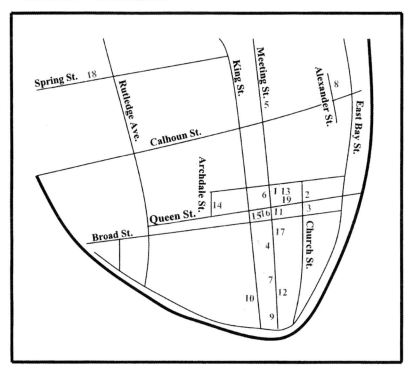

Simplified street map showing locations mentioned in text

1. Circular Congregational Church 150 Meeting St.
2. St. Philip's Episcopal Church 142 Church St.
3. French Huguenot Church 44 Queen St.
4. First Scots Presbyterian Church 53 Meeting St.
5. Charleston Museum 360 Meeting St.
6. Gibbes Museum of Art 135 Meeting St.
7. Nathaniel Russell House 51 Meeting St.
8. Liberty Tree plaque near 80 Alexander St.
9. Josiah Smith House 7 Meeting St.
10. Miles Brewton House 27 King St.
11. South Carolina Historical Society 100 Meeting St.
12. First Baptist Church 48 Meeting St.
13. Lance Hall at Circular 138 Meeting St.
14. Unitarian Church 4 Archdale St.
15. David Ramsay House 92 Broad St.
16. Hibernian Hall 105 Meeting St.
17. South Carolina Society Hall 72 Meeting St.
18. Plymouth Congregational Church 124 Spring St.
19. Green Building at Circular 138 Meeting St.

Map of peninsular Charleston, locating sites mentioned in the book. *Courtesy Lisa Hayes.*

NOTES

HISTORICAL BACKGROUND

1. Edwards, *History of the Independent Church*, 6.
2. Missildine, "Historical Sketch," 440; Edwards, *History of the Independent Church*, 7.

CHAPTER 1

3. Edwards, *History of the Independent Church*, 6.
4. McCrady, *History of South Carolina*, 376.
5. Marion, *Charleston Story*, 38.
6. Fick, *James Island Presbyterian Church*, 6.
7. Ibid., 7.
8. Edwards, *History of the Independent Church*, 16.
9. Fick, *James Island Presbyterian Church*, 6.
10. Ramsay, *History of the Independent Church*, 34.
11. Pinckney, *Thomas and Elizabeth Lamboll*, 5.
12. Edwards, *History of the Independent Church*, 17.
13. Mould and Loewe, *Historic Gravestone Art*, 87.
14. Ibid., 33.
15. Ibid., 31.
16. Ibid., 242–43.
17. Ibid., 36–37.
18. Ibid., 102.
19. Hutson, *Transactions of the Huguenot Society*, 50.
20. Burton, *South Carolina Silversmiths*, 93.
21. Mould and Loewe, *Historic Gravestone Art*, 31.
22. Miller and Andrus, *Witness to History*, 2.

23. Edwards, *History of the Independent Church*, 17.

24. CCCR, 28/689/4.

25. *1882 Yearbook of the City of Charleston*, 374–75.

Chapter 2

26. Edwards, *History of the Independent Church*, 2, 19, 20.

27. Ramsay, *History of the Independent Church*, 6.

28. Edwards, *History of the Independent Church*, 3.

29. Ibid., 22–23.

30. Jacoby, *Churches of Charleston*, 5; Edwards, *History of the Independent Church*, 20.

31. CCCR, February 5, 1775.

32. Edwards, *History of the Independent Church*, 24.

33. CCCR II, May 19, 1754.

34. Edwards, *History of the Independent Church*, 25.

35. Clarke, *Our Southern Zion*, 78–79.

36. Ibid., 79.

37. Roumillat, "Seeking Salvation," 5.

38. Ibid., 15.

39. Ibid., 5.

40. CCCR 28/689/4.

41. CCCR 28/692/19.

42. CCCR 28/692/19.

43. Mould and Loewe, *Historic Gravestone Art*, 54.

44. Clarke, *Our Southern Zion*, 104.

45. Ibid., 55.

46. Edgar, *South Carolina Encyclopedia*, 772.

47. Leland, *62 Famous Houses*, 62.

48. Mould and Loewe, *Historic Gravestone Art*, 43.

49. Edwards, *History of the Independent Church*, 36.

50. Ramsay, History of the Independent Church, vol. II, 274–75.

51. Stokes, "Presbyterian Clergy in South Carolina and the American Revolution," 270.

52. Yeadon, *History of the Circular Church*, 5.

53. Edwards, *History of the Independent Church*, 41.

54. Manual, 5; Edwards, *History of the Independent Church*, 42.

55. Mould and Loewe, *Historic Gravestone Art*, 90.

56. Walsh, *Charleston's Sons of Liberty*, 31–32.

57. Ibid., 98.

58. Manual 1870, 4.

59. Clarke, *Our Southern Zion*, 95.

60. Miller and Andrus, *Witness to History*, 21–22.

61. Yeadon, *History of the Circular Church*, 9.

62. Ibid.

63. *1882 Yearbook of the City of Charleston*, 378.

64. Manual, 5.

65. Edwards, *History of the Independent Church*, 80.

66. Shaffer, *To Be An American*, 140.

CHAPTER 3

67. Edwards, *History of the Independent Church*, 52–53.

68. Abbot, "Abiel Abbot Journals," 70.

69. Edwards, *History of the Independent Church*, 55.

70. Ibid., 144.

71. Ibid., 134.

72. Ibid., 60.

73. Ibid., 61.

74. Ibid., 62.

75. Clarke, *Our Southern Zion*, 108.

76. Ibid., 66–67.

77. Ibid., 74.

78. Ibid., 82.

79. Ibid., 104.

80. Roumillat, "Seeking Salvation," 6.

81. Clarke, *Our Southern Zion*, 29.

82. Roumillat, "Seeking Salvation," 8–20.

83. Ibid.

84. Ibid.

85. Beach papers, 43/225.

86. Edgar, *South Carolina Encyclopedia*, 436.

87. *South Carolina Historical Magazine* 63 (1957): 1-18.

88. Whitelaw and Levkoff, *Charleston Come Hell or High Water*, 129.

89. Edwards, *History of the Independent Church*, 81.

90. Ibid.

91. Marszalek, *Diary of Miss Emma Holmes*, 107.

92. Lilly and Legerton, *Historic Churches*, 79.

93. *Sunday News*, 2.

94. Edwards, *History of the Independent Church*, 83.

95. Marszalek, *Diary of Miss Emma Holmes*, 110.

96. Edwards, *History of the Independent Church*, 82.

97. Ibid.

98. Ibid., 91.

99. Ibid., 144.

100. Clarke, *Our Southern Zion*, 219.

101. Edwards, *History of the Independent Church*, 86.

102. Clarke, *Our Southern Zion*, 217.

103. Edwards, *History of the Independent Church*, 91.

104. 1870 Manual, 7.

105. Edwards, *History of the Independent Church*, 93-98.

106. Ibid.

CHAPTER 4

107. Ibid., 107.

108. Grant, "Historical Sketch," 7.

109. Jones, *Old Silver*, 115.

110. Edwards, *History of the Independent Church*, 102.

111. Ibid., 122.

112. Ibid., 114.

113. Ibid.

114. Kaye Sharpe, taped conversation at Circular Church.

115. Sharpe tape.

116. Sharpe tape.

117. Edwards, *History of the Independent Church*, 111.

118. Ibid., 147.

CHAPTER 5

119. Sloane, *Last Great Necessity*, 2.

120. Combs, *Early Gravestone Art*, 138.

121. Ibid., 54.

122. Ibid., 16.

BIBLIOGRAPHY

UNPUBLISHED RECORDS

Beach, Mary Lamboll Thomas. South Carolina Historical Society, Unpublished Letters, 1822–1825.

Circular Congregational Church Records (CCCR), located at the South Carolina Historical Society (SCHS).

Gready, Andrew P. *Record of Burials in Independent Cemetery from Miscellaneous Sources (1776–1841).* From unpublished church records.

Palmer, Benjamin M. *Funeral Records of Benjamin M. Palmer, D.D. 1815–1836.* Unpublished Circular Church Records.

Roumillat, Shelene C. "Seeking Salvation and Opportunity: Understanding African American Church Preferences in Antebellum Charleston, South Carolina." Unpublished paper for a class at Tulane University, in possession of author, 2001.

BOOKS, DISSERTATIONS, PAMPHLETS, PAPERS

Burton, E. Milby. *South Carolina Silversmiths 1690–1860.* Revised and Edited by Warren Ripley. Charleston, SC: Charleston Museum, 1942. Reprint, 1991.

Clarke, Erskine. *Our Southern Zion: A History of Calvinism in the South Carolina Low Country, 1690–1990.* Tuscaloosa: University of Alabama Press, 1996.

Combs, Diana Williams. *Early Gravestone Art in Georgia and South Carolina.* Athens: University of Georgia Press, 1986.

Cyclopedia of Eminent and Representative Men of the Carolinas of the 19th Century, vol. 1. Madison, WI: Brant & Fuller, 1892.

Edgar, Walter. *The South Carolina Encyclopedia.* Columbia: University of South Carolina Press, 2006.

Edwards, George N. *A History of the Independent or Congregational Church of Charleston, South Carolina (Commonly Known as Circular Church).* Boston: Pilgrim Press, 1947.

Fick, Sarah. *James Island Presbyterian Church, Three Hundred Years of His 1706–2006.* Charleston, SC, 2006.

Fludd, Eliza C.K. *Biographical Sketches of the Huguenot Solomon Legare.* 1886.

Grant, Henry M., Pastor. "Historical Sketch of the 'Circular' Independent or Congregational Church of Charleston, SC." Charleston: South Carolina Historical Society, 1890.

Hemphill, William Edwin. *Extracts from the Journals of the Provincial Congresses of South Carolina, 1775–1776.* Columbia: South Carolina Archives Department, 1960.

———. *The History of South Carolina, from its First Settlement in 1670 to the Year 1808.* 2 vols. Charleston, 1858.

Howe, George. *History of the Presbyterian Church in South Carolina.* Columbia: Duffie and Chapman, 1870.

Jacoby, Mary Moore. *Churches of Charleston & the Lowcountry.* Charleston, SC: The Preservation Society of Charleston, 1994.

Jones, E. Alfred. *The Old Silver of American Churches.* Letchorth, England: The Arden Press, privately printed for the National Society of Colonial Dames of America, 1913.

Keller, Albert H. "A Brief History of the Circular Church, Charleston, South Carolina." Charleston: Circular Congregational Church, 1989.

Leland, Jack. *62 Famous Houses of Charleston, South Carolina*. Charleston: A *Post & Courier* Booklet, 1989.

Lilly, Edward, ed., and Clifford L. Legerton, comp. *Historic Churches of Charleston, South Carolina*. Charleston: Legerton and Co., 1966.

Liscombe, Rhodri Windsor. *The Church Architecture of Robert Mills*. Easley, SC: Southern Historical Press, Inc., 1985.

————. *Manual of the Independent or Congregational (Circular) Church, of Charleston, S.C.* Adopted April 1870. Charleston: Walker, Evans & Cogswell, Stationers and Printers, 1870.

Marion, John Francis. *The Charleston Story: Scenes from a City's History*. Mechanicsburg, PA: Stackpole Books, 1978.

Marszalek, John F., ed. *The Diary of Miss Emma Holmes 1861–1866*. Baton Rouge: Louisiana State University Press, 1994.

McCrady, Edward. *The History of South Carolina under Proprietary Government 1670–1719*. New York: The Macmillan Company, 1902.

Middleton, Margaret Simons. *David and Martha Laurens Ramsay*. Unknown Binding. Out of Print. 1971.

Miller, Ruth M., and Ann Taylor Andrus. *Witness to History, Charleston's Old Exchange and Provost Dungeon*. Orangeburg, SC: Sandlapper Publishing, Inc., 1986.

Missildine, A.H. "Historical Sketch of the Independent or Congregational (Circular) Church, from its origin to the present time. Selected from the most reliable sources." Written for the *1882 Yearbook of the City of Charleston*.

Mould, David R., and Missy Loewe. *Historic Gravestone Art of Charleston, South Carolina, 1695–1802*. Jefferson, NC: McFarland and Company, Inc., 2006.

Pinckney, Elise. *Thomas and Elizabeth Lamboll: Early Charleston Gardeners.* Charleston: Charleston Museum, 1969.

Poston, Jonathan H., for Historic Charleston foundation. *The Buildings of Charleston—A Guide to the City's Architecture.* Columbia: University of South Carolina Press, 1997.

Ramsay, David, MD. *The History of the Independent or Congregational Church in Charleston, South Carolina, from its origin till the year 1814; with an Appendix, 1815.* Philadelphia: printed for the author by J. Maxwell, 1815.

Salley, A.S. *Death Notices in the* South Carolina Gazette, *1732–1775.* Columbia: The State Co., 1917.

Shaffer, Arthur H. *To Be An American—David Ramsay and the Making of the American Consciousness.* Columbia: University of South Carolina Press, 1991.

Sloane, David Charles. *The Last Great Necessity—Cemeteries in American History.* Baltimore: Johns Hopkins University Press, 1995.

Walsh, Richard. *Charleston's Sons of Liberty, A Study of the Artisans, 1763–1789.* Columbia: University of South Carolina Press, 1968.

Way, William. *History of the New England Society of Charleston, South Carolina, 1810–1919.* 1920. Digitalized 15 May, 2006.

Webber, Mabel L. *Death Notices in the South Carolina Gazette, 1776–1774.* Columbia: The State Co., 1917.

Whitelaw, T.S., and Alice F. Levkoff. *Charleston Come Hell or High Water.* Charleston: Alice F. Levkoff and Patti F. Whitelaw, n.d.

Yeadon, Richard, Esq. *History of the Circular Church, Its Origin, Building, Rebuilding, and Recent Ornamental Renovation.* Published in the *Charleston Courier,* July 16, 1853. Appendices: "Continuation of the History of the Circular Church," by Rev. Benjamin M. Palmer, DD; "Continuation of the History of the Circular Church," by Bazile Lanneau, Esq.

ARTICLES

Abbot, Abiel. "The Abiel Abbot Journals." *South Carolina Historical Magazine* 68 (1967). November 1818 historical notes from a Yankee preacher's journal after a visit to Charleston.

Barnhart, Mrs. William. "Inscriptions from the Independent or Congregational (Circular) Church Yard, Charleston, SC." *South Carolina Historical and Genealogical Magazine* 69 (1968): 253–61.

Bedford, Rev. Archie B. "A Church with a History: Circular Church in Charleston, South Carolina observes it 275th anniversary throughout 1956." Reprinted from *Advance*, December 28, 1955.

Guillard, Thomas. "The Old Circular Church—A Venerable Landmark that is Passing Away." *Sunday News*, February 19, 1888.

Hutson, Michael Jenkins. *Transactions of the Huguenot Society of South Carolina* no. 5 (1897): 50.

Hutson, Mrs. R.W. "Register kept by the Rev. Wm. Hutson of Stony Creek Independent Congregational Church and (Circular) Congregational Church in Charleston SC 1743–1760." *South Carolina Historical and Genealogical Magazine* 38 (1937): 21–36.

———. *Transactions of the Huguenot Society of South Carolina*, No. 895 (1884): 49–58.

Stokes, Durward T. "The Presbyterian Clergy in South Carolina and the American Revolution." *South Carolina Historical Magazine* 71 (1970).

Webber, Mabel L. "Inscriptions from the Independent or Congregational (Circular) Church Yard. Charleston, SC." *South Carolina Historical and Genealogical Magazine* 29 (1928), 55–66, 133–56, 238–57, 306–28; 38 (1937): 142–45.

———. "Josiah Smith's Diary 1780–1781." *South Carolina Historical and Genealogical Magazine* 33 (1932): 1–28, 79–116, 197–207, 281–89; 34 (1933): 31–39, 67–84, 138–48, 194–210.

———. "Records Kept by Colonel Isaac Hayne." *South Carolina Historical and Genealogical Magazine* 10 (1909): 146–70, 220–35; 11 (1910): 27–38, 92–106; 12 (1911): 160–70.

INTERNET SOURCES

http://www.citadel.edu/library/Knob/knob_m.htm
(Sources: "In Memoriam—Andrew Buist Murray," *Charleston Year Book*, 1929, 349–52; Prioleau Reading Room JS13.C33 1929; "Andrew Murray, Philanthropist, has Passed Away," *News and Courier*, December 21, 1928, 1, 11)

http://famous.adoption.com/famous/murray-andrew-buist.html

http://www.scottishritecalifornia.org/charleston_street's_continued.htm

INDEX

Visit us at
www.historypress.net